Praise for *Already Here*

"Already Here is *an awe-inspiring after-death communication received by a medical doctor from his son Christopher who had crossed over after a fatal accident. Soon after, signs began to appear and Chris began speaking to his father, imparting his knowledge and wisdom about the purpose of life. This inspiring book is an education for living—about how to enjoy life to its fullest, transforming anger and hate into love, about being human, and how love transcends physical death.*"

— **Anita Moorjani**, *New York Times* best-selling author
of *Dying to Be Me* and *What If This Is Heaven?*

"*Dr. Leo Galland, a respected global leader in the field of holistic medicine, has written an astounding book of revelations about the nature of heaven and earth, loss and pain, and love. All guided by the spirit of his special-needs son, Chris, who died at the age of 22. I read the entire book in one unforgettable afternoon and was profoundly moved. You don't want to miss this one.*"

— **Christiane Northrup, M.D.**,
#1 *New York Times* best-selling author

"*Leo Galland brings us on a journey of the heart, infinite awareness, and discovery.*"

— **Deepak Chopra, M.D.**, author of *You Are the Universe*

"*A gripping and triumphant story. Part intimate memoir, part spiritual guidebook, Dr. Galland's heartfelt chronicle is a spellbinding exploration of life after death, and a bracing reminder of the indestructible power of a father's love. At one point in the story, Dr. Galland underscores the impact Christopher had on his family, recalling his brother once saying, 'I really need a dose of Christopher.' Just one day after finishing this remarkable and inspiring book, I found myself longing for another dose of Christopher too.*"

— **Marlo Thomas**, award-winning actress, producer, activist,
and best-selling author of *Free to Be . . . You and Me*

Already Here

ALSO BY DR LEO GALLAND

The Allergy Solution (with Jonathan Galland, J.D.)*
The Fat Resistance Diet (with Jonathan Galland, J.D.)
Power Healing
Superimmunity for Kids

*Available from Hay House
Please visit:

Hay House UK: www.hayhouse.co.uk
Hay House USA: www.hayhouse.com®
Hay House Australia: www.hayhouse.com.au
Hay House India: www.hayhouse.co.in

* * *

Already Here

A Doctor Discovers
the Truth about Heaven

DR LEO GALLAND

HAY HOUSE

Carlsbad, California • New York City
London • Sydney • New Delhi

Published in the United Kingdom by:
Hay House UK Ltd, Astley House, 33 Notting Hill Gate, London W11 3JQ
Tel: +44 (0)20 3675 2450; Fax: +44 (0)20 3675 2451; www.hayhouse.co.uk

Published in the United States of America by:
Hay House Inc., PO Box 5100, Carlsbad, CA 92018-5100
Tel: (1) 760 431 7695 or (800) 654 5126
Fax: (1) 760 431 6948 or (800) 650 5115; www.hayhouse.com

Published in Australia by:
Hay House Australia Ltd, 18/36 Ralph St, Alexandria NSW 2015
Tel: (61) 2 9669 4299; Fax: (61) 2 9669 4144; www.hayhouse.com.au

Published in India by:
Hay House Publishers India, Muskaan Complex, Plot No.3, B-2,
Vasant Kunj, New Delhi 110 070
Tel: (91) 11 4176 1620; Fax: (91) 11 4176 1630; www.hayhouse.co.in

A catalogue record for this book is available from the British Library.

Tradepaper ISBN: 978-1-78817-003-1
Hardback ISBN: 978-1-4019-5416-1
E-book ISBN: 978-1-4019-5417-8
Audiobook ISBN: 978-1-4019-5592-2

Interior composition: Greg Johnson/Textbook Perfect
Cover design: Kathleen Lynch
Cover image: Radius Images/Alamy Stock Photos
Photo of Christopher: Christina Galland

Grateful acknowledgement is made to the Free to Be Foundation to
reprint lyrics from 'Free to Be... You and Me'.

Printed by CPI Group (UK) Ltd, Croydon CR0 4YY

For Nell, Christopher's Grandma,
whose love and patience had no limit

Contents

Christopher

Prologue

Already Here describes the death of my son, Christopher, at the age of 22, the direct evidence of life after death that he showed me, and the communication I had with him after his death, which totally changed my understanding of the universe, of life and its meaning, and of Heaven.

In life, Christopher was a brain-damaged special-needs child who challenged everyone he knew with his unpredictable behavior and uncanny insights. After his death, he revealed to me the real purpose of his life: to be a spiritual master who taught others by confounding their assumptions and expectations. He showed me that the human soul is indestructible and that the universe depends for its existence on the immortality of individual consciousness, because the universe itself is an act of love.

Christopher's wisdom was revealed to me in three gifts, which I call the Gift of the Opposite, the Gift of Presence, and the Gift of Timelessness. I came to realize that these gifts were not intended for me alone. They contain ancient wisdom, held sacred in many traditions, and Chris intended for me to share them with others. *Already Here* was written under his direction.

CHAPTER

1

My heart was pounding. I could barely stand. A hollow, buzzing noise filled my head, echoing the dreadful message.

"There's been an accident," Imelda had said. "A hospital in Massachusetts called for you. It's about Christopher. He's in the emergency room and they're doing resuscitation. The doctor wants you to call."

"When did this happen?" I asked. I felt as if this were a dream or a movie. Words were being spoken, some of them came from my lips, but they had no relationship to me.

"They called ten minutes ago. He was hiking in the woods. There was an accident. An ambulance came . . ."

Despite the panic those words evoked, my hand was steady as I dialed the hospital's number and my voice was calm as I spoke. Half my mind saw Christopher on a stretcher, white coats crowded round, their hands on his chest, rhythmically pounding . . . an intravenous line in place . . . a cardiac monitor. I had seen this so many times, had been among the white coats, but always with a stranger on the stretcher.

What does this mean for you, Chris? I cried in silence. *Further brain damage? Greater neurological impairment? The loss of everything you've worked so hard for? Life in a coma? Or a miraculous recovery? A paradoxical gain in brain function, reversing the handicaps with which you've lived for twenty-two years?* A deluge of conflicting, confusing images, of unspeakable fears and fantastic wishes, flooded my brain. None of it cracked my professional veneer.

"This is Dr. Leo Galland. I'm calling from New York, about my son."

"We're not sure what happened," explained the emergency room physician. "He was on a hike with some people from North Plain Farm. They found him lying facedown in a shallow stream. There was so much cold water in his lungs, the paramedics had a hard time establishing an airway. Water just gushed out through the endotracheal tube. I understand he has a seizure disorder. He might have had a seizure, fallen into the stream, and aspirated cold water. We've been working on him for about twenty minutes. There's been no pulse and his EKG is flat. His temperature on arrival was really low, only sixty-eight degrees, probably because of the cold water in his lungs. We've warmed him up to eighty degrees. What do you want us to do?"

"Don't stop yet," I pleaded, knowing that hypothermia protects the brain. "Keep warming him and continue the resuscitation, please. Let's see what happens when his temperature rises some more. I'll be waiting here by the phone."

I sat by the reception desk. My limbs were leaden, my field of vision blurred, hornets still buzzing in my head. "What's the afternoon schedule like?" I asked Imelda. She showed me the appointment book.

"Most of these patients live or work in Manhattan," I said as I looked it over. "Please reschedule them. Roberta Singer is coming in at two, from Tom's River. I'd better see her. It's a long trip; we can't just send her home. She should be here in a few minutes. Send her in as soon as she arrives. And let me know the moment Christina returns. I have to tell her about this myself. I don't think Christopher is going to live."

Roberta Singer was right on time for her appointment, her second visit. I looked at her. I looked down at her chart. I was supposed to review the results of laboratory tests, provide a meaningful interpretation, and suggest treatment. As hard as I tried, I could not make sense of the numbers in front of me.

"I'm sorry," I said to her. "I can't continue today. About fifteen minutes ago, I received a phone call from a hospital. My son had an accident and his heart stopped beating. He's undergoing cardiac resuscitation now. I just can't concentrate."

The words were hard for me to speak. I had never asked a patient to understand my problems or share my pain. I had never stepped out of the role of doctor, even when admitting a failure or a mistake. I had always been ready to listen, to learn, to respond actively. Some irrational part of me thought I should still be in control, even now. But I wasn't.

"I'm so sorry," replied Roberta. "My problems are not terribly important. They can wait."

As she left the room, Imelda called me on the intercom to tell me that my wife had arrived: "Christina has just entered the building. She's getting on the elevator."

I walked quickly to the reception area. My mind spun in circles as I searched for the words with which I would break this news to my wife. As soon as she entered the office, she'd know something was wrong. I had to be the one who told her.

Her cheerful smile disappeared when she saw my face. She followed me into the back hallway. "Christopher's in the hospital," I said, holding her in my arms. "He had an accident and they're resuscitating him."

She squeezed me tightly, her fingers digging into my back. I couldn't see her face, but I could feel the tears on my cheek and hear the terror in her voice. "Don't tell me what happened. I don't want to know."

We stood, embracing one another, and cried in silence for several minutes. Then we went into my consultation room and collapsed on the chairs that faced my desk, staring silently at the window. There was nothing to say, nothing to do except to wait, numbed, frozen in time and space by the weight of a tragedy unfolding three hours away, totally beyond our influence or control. A curious thought wandered through my consciousness: I had never sat in this chair; I was always on the other side, behind the desk.

The air felt as heavy as my limbs.

Then a sudden feeling of electricity parted the heaviness. We stood up, suddenly aroused. The room felt supercharged, as if lightning were about to strike. The room was gone. My eyes saw nothing, but my mind was filled with a pure white light.

"Christopher is here," gasped Christina. "He's so bright!"

A shape emerged from the light, the smiling face of a robust young man with blond hair, radiating joy. He seemed to rise up, powerfully and majestically. The contours of his body were vague . . . no arms or legs or neck could be clearly seen, just an oblong shape, rising, with a beautiful glowing face at its apex. The face was Christopher's, but perfect, with none of the scars left by his many mishaps. The sense of joy, freedom, and strength radiating from him exceeded anything I had ever experienced or imagined.

Christina and I had exactly the same vision. We had entered a place where space and time didn't matter, where inside and outside didn't matter. The brilliance of Christopher's presence overwhelmed everything. His intense happiness took our breath away. What was most astonishing about this vision was not its appearance, but the sensation of sublime bliss and limitless power that flowed from Christopher's being. It was like watching an immense explosion that was totally controlled and destroyed nothing.

Then it was over. Christina and I were standing in my office; the light was dim, the air was still, and the phone was ringing.

"He's gone," we both said at the same time, quite clear about the double meaning.

I answered the phone, knowing exactly what I would hear. On the other end was Dr. Greene from the emergency room.

"I'm sorry, but his temperature is up to ninety-two degrees and nothing's happening; there's no electrical activity in the heart."

"Thank you for trying," I said. "You can stop now."

I turned to Christina. "That was unbelievable. Chris was so . . . happy!"

"He was so full of light and so strong."

We hugged each other and cried, overwhelmed by a confusion of feeling, of grief and joy, loss and gain.

"How wonderful that he came to us," sobbed Christina. "How lucky we are. When I stepped off the elevator and I saw the look on your face and you said you had something to tell me, I couldn't stand it. I didn't feel that I could live. Not that I didn't want to live. I felt that I couldn't, that I would just . . . die with him. So he came here. How incredible. How many millions of people lose their children and suffer and never see what we just saw?"

Christina had not the slightest doubt about the truth of our visitation. I was shaken to the very core of my being. Had I imagined it? Was this a shared hallucination? Or was this the *real* Christopher? Was there something like that within me? Within everyone? A being of power and purity and unearthly joy? A literal Spirit, outlasting the body, discarding it the way a butterfly sheds a cocoon?

"We both saw him," I said softly. "Christopher always was amazing. I never knew how amazing."

She moved away from me and sat down. Her voice hardened. "This doesn't mean it's all right, you know. I don't ever want to hear anyone say that Chris is better off being dead. He loved being himself. I can't stand having him gone. He was so looking forward to Thanksgiving."

CHAPTER

2

It's hard to say exactly how Christopher's visitation affected our grief over his death. Without it, I think we would have been crushed by the incompleteness of his life, suddenly severed by his bizarre drowning. Despite the vision we'd had, we had no lasting feeling of joy or triumph or relief. We had to explain Chris's death to his brothers, and that was the hardest task of all.

Chris had been the second of triplets, born prematurely, weighing barely more than two pounds. Jonathan and Jefferson had thrived and grown into healthy, vigorous, and gifted children. Chris had suffered brain injury shortly after birth, apparently from an episode of apnea, which left him developmentally disabled and prone to seizures. Despite his disabilities, he had become remarkable in his own unique ways: in the flashes of humor and poetry and insight that graced his speech; in his total fascination with every mechanical or electrical device ever invented and his ability to break anything in the blink of an eye, no matter how closely he was watched; in his boundless capacity for love and forgiveness and his inexhaustible propensity to try the patience of everyone who knew him, except his grandmother. In Christopher's world, no person was to be left untested, no limit was to be left intact. He loved it that way, and no reward or punishment could change it.

The possible adverse consequences of his behavior fascinated Chris in the same way that knobs and latches did. He would do anything just to see the effect—with one exception. He would do nothing mean or hurtful to others, and if he sensed in any way that his provocative behavior caused another person pain rather than mere anger or annoyance, he would stop. As for rewards, they all seemed rather petty to him. Sure, he loved his mom's pancakes, his grandma's cookies, the roller coaster at Lake Compounce, and watching the Muppets. But the one thing that Chris most wanted was the one thing he could never have: to be like his brothers, attend the same school, play the same sports.

The most memorable aspect of Chris's bad behavior was the deliberation that he brought to it. One Sunday morning when Chris was about 10, he awakened us at the crack of dawn, demanding attention.

"Chris, it's still dark," I said to him. "Go back to bed."

"I want you to get up," he said flatly.

"I'm tired, Chris. I want to sleep some more. Now go back to your bed."

He looked quickly around the bedroom. "If you don't get up," he insisted, "I'll touch everything I see." He quickly catalogued the items on the dresser in front of him. "I'll touch . . . the money . . . the glasses . . . the phone . . ." Then he laughed and laughed.

A school psychologist once described Chris as engaging in some form of attention-getting behavior at least every five minutes. It could be maddening, but there were always ways of getting Chris to stop, if you didn't let your own anger at him get in the way. There were many times when I realized how irrational it was to get angry at Chris, because my own anger only fed his oppositional nature and made it more obstinate. I would feel very smart at having understood this, and then I would get angry anyway. No matter how smart I was, Chris could show me that I was pretty stupid underneath it all. Eventually I would recognize that Chris was destined to test everyone he knew to the limits of their endurance and to totally destroy the myths they had created about themselves. If you thought you were a reasonable and mature person, Chris could drive you out of control. If you thought you were kind and good, Chris could bring out your violence and hostility. And if you thought you were a loser, Chris could show you that you were an effective human being. He had a genius for sensing and confounding people's ideas about themselves.

Chris was a paradox in many other ways. He lived a very difficult life, full of disappointment and heartbreak. There were so many things he wanted to be able to do, because his brothers did them, but that he was incapable of doing. Yet he never showed a trace of bitterness or self-pity. He loved being himself. He was proud of being Christopher. Not because of anything he did or accomplished, but simply because he *was*.

He felt the same way about other people also. When he went to school, he was glad to see each and every pupil and member of the staff. He would stand in the doorway and shout, "Hello, I'm back!" He didn't care if someone was inarticulate, strapped into a wheelchair rocking back and forth, and unaware of his presence. That person was an individual to Chris and he would pay him the respect of an individual "hello." He didn't care if someone was pretty or ugly, rich or poor, generous or miserly—they were all the same. Not because he didn't *recognize* the difference, but because it didn't matter to him.

Although Chris encountered a number of mean and angry people during his life, he never held a grudge. If someone had been physically abusive, Chris might avoid him—or provoke him—but Chris would never stay angry at him. Not because his memory was bad; Chris remembered everything, especially broken promises. I have never known anyone with Chris's capacity to forgive.

When Chris finished his schooling, at the age of 21, he went to live at North Plain Farm in Great Barrington, a small community created as an outgrowth of the Camphill movement, which had started in England. The basis of the community was "Lifesharing." People with developmental and intellectual disabilities lived and worked together along with their helpers, sharing their lives. Growth came from each person's effort in building community.

Lifesharing is grounded in the philosophy of Rudolf Steiner, the Austrian educator and visionary who founded the Waldorf School movement. In 1906, at the age of 40, Steiner startled the academic world by publicly describing his psychic experiences—a shocking revelation from an acclaimed scholar. He spent the next two and a half decades building a series of international movements to apply his spiritual insights to education, agriculture, and the healing arts. Personally, I had found Steiner's writings to be difficult and esoteric and his views on health care to be mystifying. But I was impressed by the practical achievements of his educational philosophy and felt great respect for those individuals who were attempting to apply it.

There were three small farms near Great Barrington in addition to North Plain that were part of the Lifesharing community: Buena Vista Farm, Orchard House, and Shadowood. The total community numbered about 40 people.

Needless to say, Christopher's bottomless individualism was a profound challenge to the whole community, and the demands of Lifesharing were a profound challenge to Christopher.

Chris rose to the challenge, but he never stopped tempting fate. Six weeks before his death, while working at a cooperative garden near Orchard House, Chris climbed into one of the group's minivans, which was parked on the edge of a hill. Placing himself in the driver's seat, he released the emergency brake and shifted into neutral. The van rolled off the shoulder of the road and through the fields. It careened down a quarter mile of pasture and came to rest in a clump of bushes at the bottom of a hill. Miraculously, Chris was unhurt and the van was barely scratched. Chris didn't speak a word for two hours afterward. A few days later, on a visit to the farm, Christina asked him why he had taken the van. He beamed his ear-to-ear grin and said triumphantly, "I wanted to drive!"

During his nine months at North Plain Farm, Christopher's conquest of himself became a focal point for the growth and cohesiveness of the community. If he could trust the group enough to relinquish his constant testing of limits, then the community itself was validated. By the time of his death, he had crossed the threshold and a new era for Chris seemed at hand. Death suddenly destroyed the possibility of going further.

"It's a tragedy," said Jonathan with quiet anger when we told him about Christopher's death. "His life was tragic and so is his death. It's too painful to talk about." Jon had been fiercely protective of his brother ever since the age of two, when he first perceived that Chris was different. He had no interest in the story of our visit from Chris's Spirit, nor did Jeff. Two weeks earlier, the two had gone to Great Barrington to spend a weekend with Chris. As he planned the trip, Jon had said to us, "I really need a dose of Christopher." The phrase stuck: "a dose of Christopher." It was the way Jon remembered his brother:

ingenuous, direct, and a constant threat to the hypocrisy of convention. As one example, Chris took his holidays seriously. On Easter or at Christmastime, he would walk down the street or through a mall, introducing himself to people and wishing them well, whether they wanted to acknowledge him or not. "Happy Easter," he would say. "I'm Chris. I hope you have a nice holiday." "Merry Christmas. I'm Chris. Can I shake your hand?" For Jon, *that* was the real Christopher, not a ghost.

Only Jordan, our youngest child, not yet nine years old, accepted the story of Chris's visit. He and Chris had been very close. Jordan would never forget how Chris would embrace him and shriek, "You're my little brother!" He knew through and through that Christopher's Spirit was immortal. When he saw his mother crying and clutching Chris's picture, he placed his arms around her neck. Christina sobbed, "I can't believe that this is my life, without Christopher in it."

Jordan responded, with complete certainty, "Don't worry, Mommy, he's *fine*."

CHAPTER

3

As we wrestled with the heart-wrenching task of telling everyone in the family that Christopher had died, the vision of Chris's amazing Spirit seemed more and more elusive. I turned to it many times a day, trying to relive every second of the experience, as if it were a drug to chase away despair and anger.

I had no doubt about what I'd seen. I felt blessed that we'd been given this vision of paradise. But I had no idea how to process it. I didn't realize that Christopher wasn't done with me yet, and that by the time he finished, he would turn my worldview upside down and challenge everything I thought I knew about myself or about him. He'd give us another demonstration of the immortality of his soul that was even more compelling than what we'd seen, and he'd show me that the immortality of each individual soul is intimately connected to the origin of the universe.

I'd been trained as a scientist and researcher. Logic, reason, and experimentation were my most important tools. For most of my life I had considered the great mysteries of life to be essentially unknowable: how we came to be here, for what reason or purpose—if any—and what happens after death. In high school, I'd been impressed by the writings of Thomas Aquinas, who drew a hard line, never to be crossed, between knowledge and faith. What one could *know*, reasoned Aquinas, did not require faith. Religion was based on faith, not knowledge; hence the truths of religious faith could only be believed, never confirmed as fact. By their very nature and God's intent, they were beyond proving. Not being one to take anything on faith, I had dismissed religion and spiritual matters as fanciful and committed myself to a lifetime of agnostic thinking, applying the skepticism of science to all beliefs. The results of skepticism were paradoxical, however.

I found it easy to believe, as do most scientists, that life arose completely by chance: the right environmental conditions, the proper ingredients in a primordial chemical soup, the random association of molecules assembling the primitive nucleotides of the genetic code, a billion years of evolution yielding the human brain, the chemistry of which created consciousness. The problem with this point of view is that it is not truly scientific. It requires a surreptitious leap of faith.

In his book *The Astonishing Hypothesis: The Scientific Search for the Soul*, Sir Francis Crick, the renowned physicist and biochemist who received the Nobel Prize for his work in unraveling the structure of DNA, states the "scientific" view of the human soul quite succinctly: "'You,' your joys and your sorrows, your memories and your ambitions, your sense of personal identity and free will, are in fact no more than the behavior of a vast assembly of nerve cells and their associated molecules."[1] And: "If the scientific facts are sufficiently striking and well-established, and if they appear to support the Astonishing Hypothesis, then it will be possible to argue that the idea that man has a disembodied soul is . . . unnecessary."[2] Over the next decade, until his death in 2004, Crick continued to work on a theory of human consciousness as the by-product of chemistry and anatomy. No soul, no spirit, just molecular networks.

Crick's hypothesis is a shining example of scientific reductionism, the belief that the best way to understand anything is to break it down into its component parts and study them. His theories expose the scientist's leap of faith in a most flagrant form. Between descriptions of the physiology and psychology of vision, which make up the bulk of Crick's evidence, and anything that could reasonably represent an approach to understanding human consciousness, let alone a soul, lies a vast intellectual chasm. In 1994, Crick had to admit, rather sheepishly: "At the moment of writing, there does not appear to be one set of ideas that click together in a convincing way to make a detailed neural hypothesis that has the smell of

[1] Francis Crick, *The Astonishing Hypothesis: The Scientific Search for the Soul* (New York: Charles Scribner's Sons, 1994), 1.
[2] Ibid., 261.

being correct. If you think I appear to be groping my way through the jungle you are quite right."[3] After thousands of hours delving into visual processing by monkeys, Crick summed up his progress by stating that he studied vision because it was easier and that he had to leave aside "the more difficult aspects of consciousness, such as emotion and self-consciousness."[4]

What assumptions would allow Crick to express his theory of the soul as if it carried behind it the awesome power of "science"? First was his *opinion* that in reducing a human being to the essential components, scientists could stop at the molecules that make up the body. Second was his unstated decision to limit the field of inquiry to measurable, replicable phenomena, and to assume that what is learned there can be extended to phenomena that are not measurable and cannot be experimentally replicated. Third was his high regard for "the spectacular advance of modern science," which has allowed us to know much that was at one time considered unknowable. These are *opinions*, and although they are shared by many scientists, they are no less subjective than the opinions that underlie most types of spiritual belief. Over the next several years, as I investigated Christopher's revelations, I realized that these "spectacular advances" have been accompanied by a loss of vision. There are truths we rarely see because we've lost the ability to see them.

But I'm getting ahead of myself.

---

[3] Crick, *The Astonishing Hypothesis*, 251.
[4] Francis Crick and Christof Koch, "A Framework for Consciousness," *Nature Neuroscience* 6 (2003): 119–126.

Following Christopher's visitation, I concluded that it was more in keeping with the spirit of science to forgo opinions based on reductionist thinking and to be skeptical about the unsupported assertions of scientists. Without faith, but with just enough doubt about the soundness of conventional thinking, I was prepared to be open to experience and the lessons it would teach me. I expected that the questions would exceed the answers—that I would search more than I would find and sow more than I would reap. I was wrong.

Over the next three weeks, Christopher would reveal to me far more about the nature of life than I ever expected. My dead, brain-damaged, 22-year-old son would show me, with about as much evidence as I could reasonably expect, that death is not the end of life, but merely a turning point in the adventure of the individual Spirit. And once I thought I had that down, he'd turn my understanding on its head and give me a vision of the universe that would completely shatter my notion of what is real.

CHAPTER

4

We decided that Chris should be buried in the Berkshires, in Great Barrington, so that the community with which he had shared the last months of his life, and on which his death had such an impact, could say its farewell. On Thursday, November 3, in a dreary November rain, we drove to the farm, which is about 150 miles north of New York City. The funeral was to be on Saturday. There were two days for preparation and two nights for community meetings to celebrate Chris with word and song.

North Plain Farm was 10 acres of woods and pasture in the midst of a large plain north of the town of Great Barrington. The main house was a white clapboard colonial, built around 1830, sitting directly on North Plain Road, and flanked by barns and sheds and sheep pens, some old and weathered, some new and brightly painted. A stream ran alongside the muddy, unpaved driveway.

Numerous additions popped up from the back of the old colonial, stuck on to one another like dominos, leading back from the original kitchen and family room with its ancient stone fireplace, tall and shallow, to the new, modern kitchen that the community was still building. Chris had worked on the kitchen. He had delighted in breaking up an old concrete slab with a jackhammer. He had learned to hammer nails straight into two-by-fours and to line up the beams. He had planted forsythia by the side of the driveway. He had learned about life on a farm. Chris learned to feed the sheep and goats and to pen them up at night. He saw a lambing in the spring and watched the lamb grow day by day. He helped nurse a baby goat whose mother had died.

When Chris first came to the farm, animals held no interest for him. They couldn't be provoked the way that humans could be. They never said "Stop!" or "Don't do that!" They didn't care what he broke or if he changed the channels on the radio or wanted a different dessert than everyone else. He had largely ignored our family dog and had slept through trips to the zoo. One afternoon, as we walked with Chris and Jordan through the grounds of the Bronx Zoo, we had seen the North American brown bears putting on a rare show in their outdoor habitat. Instead of sleeping in a hidden alcove of rock, the male bears stood erect, eight feet tall on hind legs, growling, snarling, and slapping one another, then wrestling and tumbling in a mating contest. Christina and I stood transfixed by the awesome display of strength and agility. Christopher welcomed the respite from walking, taking the opportunity to sit on a bench and grab a nap.

Christina awakened him and showed him the acrobatics of the bears. "Look, Chris," she cajoled him, "isn't that amazing? Look at how big and strong and fast those animals are." He didn't care. "What kind of animals are those, Chris? You've seen pictures of them before. These are real." He looked away. "Come on, Chris, what are those animals?"

"Pigs!" he groaned, to shut her up.

If animals bored Chris, walking repelled him. He was good for a hundred feet, then he wanted to stop and rest. Running was another matter. He could run continuously, especially when he was supposed to walk, or at least when he was not supposed to run. When he spied his mom at the other end of a playing field during the Special Olympics, he'd be off like a shot in her direction.

When he first came to the farm, Chris refused to hike in the woods. One reason may have been that he was taking such high doses of medication for seizure control that he was drowsy a good part of the day. Meals would also make him sleepy. He seemed to have a kind of food sensitivity, possibly to preservatives or other additives. He loved fast-food restaurants, especially McDonald's and Roy Rogers. A meal at Roy Rogers was guaranteed to put him to sleep within 15 minutes. On a diet of farm vegetables and home-baked bread, free-range chicken and lamb stew, Chris slowly emerged from the stupor that had shrouded his days. The dose of medication for seizures had been lowered, without any increase in their frequency or severity. With the encouragement of the other residents, he began to participate in group hikes in the Berkshires, ascending a ridge and returning, a distance of about two miles, sometimes walking in the front of the group. How ironic that a hike in the woods should have killed him.

Great Barrington is a sleepy New England town flanking the Housatonic River. Its center is built around a cluster of elegant churches, separated from one another by small shops. The side streets are lined with white clapboard houses. At both ends of Main Street, the town dissolves, either into fields and meadows or into small shopping malls with large parking lots.

On Friday morning, we drove into town to make plans for a Requiem Mass at the Church of St. Peter, an impressive structure of gray stone and neo-Gothic lines, with stained-glass windows, a handsome pipe organ, and a balcony for the choir. I was not a religious person, but I had no doubt that to process Christopher's death we needed all the tradition and ritual there was. We inquired at the church office. The church was available on Saturday afternoon and the pastor wouldn't mind if a priest from out of town who was a family friend came to say the Mass. If we supplied our own singers, the church could supply an organist.

The funeral home was naturally enough in the center of town, near the church. St. Peter's Cemetery was across the river, behind Four Brothers Pizza. It seemed like a good resting place. Chris loved pizza. He especially loved this restaurant because of its name, which seemed to announce for all to see that this place was meant for Christopher and his three brothers.

The florist we chose was located just behind the church. As we entered the shop, a young woman walked out with red and blue helium-filled balloons. I was seized by an irresistible impulse.

"Let's get balloons," I said to Christina. "Twenty-two bright yellow balloons. We'll release them by the side of the grave."

As soon as I said it, I had misgivings. Where did that idea come from? Was that a responsible thing to do?

"Yes," said Christina, reading my mind. "That's how I feel about Chris. Rising up, bright, like a yellow balloon."

The decision to order balloons gave us a bounce. Making all the other arrangements left us exhausted. Every little thing that a parent must do to bury a child seems to carry with it the weight of the world. When you feel as if it requires all your energy to live from one day to the next, you have to make decisions about things like burial plots and coffins and music. And yet we wanted to make those decisions, because we wanted the Mass and funeral to be a tribute to Christopher's life, not merely a ritual for expressing the recognition of his death.

We called Father Gerry Fitzsimmons, a priest and missionary in the Montfort order. Fitz had grown up in the same part of Queens as Christina and had been a parish priest in Port Jefferson, New York, when I was on the medical faculty of Stony Brook University, a few miles away. He had given Jon and Jeff their First Communion, and later he had traveled to Connecticut to baptize Jordan and to Long Island to bury Christina's grandmother. As a missionary, Fitz was accustomed to traveling, giving missions at churches that requested him. Many did, and they usually asked him back. The surprise was that Fitz had no mission scheduled for Saturday and said he would gladly come up to preach at Chris's Mass.

We called Margaret and Peter Cymanow, friends from Manhattan and musicians. The Cymanows were Polish immigrants who met in Kraków. Margaret had the purest, most moving soprano I have ever heard. Peter's response brought tears to my eyes: "We will be very happy to sing for Christopher." They would bring their friend Wojtek, who sings bass, and their two sons, Paavo and Shimon, who were playmates of Jordan's. We selected the music together: "Amazing Grace" as the processional, Mozart's "Ave Verum Corpus" for Communion, Schubert's "Ave Maria" before the sermon, Bardos's mournful "Eli, Eli, Lamma Sabacthani?" for the recessional.

The two evenings before the funeral were filled with communal dinners, one night at North Plain and one night at the funeral home. We talked about Christopher, we lit his prayer candle, and we sang together, folk songs and spirituals, especially the two that Chris had liked best, "Ezekiel Saw the Wheel" and "This Little Light of Mine."

Christina and I spoke with people who were particularly close to Christopher. There were two, Luke and Daniel, young men in their early 20s on whom Chris had a striking impact. I'll share their stories later. What I learned about them as I prepared to write this book radically changed my understanding of Chris's life.

CHAPTER

5

Chris's funeral was Saturday morning. This was the saddest day. Wednesday we had been stunned by Chris's death and the vision of his Spirit. Thursday and Friday had been filled with travel, preparation, meetings, and the sharing of stories. Saturday was the time for burial, a task so melancholy it left room for no feeling but grief.

It had rained for two days. Now the weather was just raw. Gusts of wind stirred up the fallen oak leaves scattered over the farmhouse lawn. Gray clouds filled the sky, swirling with the wind. From time to time they would break ranks and allow a patch of blue sky to shine through, but only for a moment. The hearse was waiting in front of the church, the dark-brown wood coffin resting on the sidewalk beside it, closed. Christina cried uncontrollably at its sight. Flanked by Jordan and Grandma, she walked slowly into the church. I had not yet seen Father Fitzsimmons or the Cymanows. I hoped they had arrived. The funeral director asked for the pallbearers.

I grabbed a brass handle at the rear corner of the coffin and lifted, in unison with Jeff, Jon, and Luke. Its weight came as a shock.

It's unbelievably heavy, I thought. *Oh my God, this is Christopher's weight. This is my son's body that I'm lifting.*

A sharp stabbing pain pierced my right side, below the armpit. It hurt to breathe. I had pulled an intercostal muscle. I stiffened all the muscles on the right side of my chest as a splint for the one I had just torn, ignored the pain, and kept carrying the coffin up the walkway, up the front steps of the church, into the foyer. I was surprised to see a cluster of yellow balloons hovering by the doorway. They were a strange sight, tied by yellow ribbons to a sandbag, filling a space the size of a large holly bush, looking like a fantastical plant from the dream of a child. I had expected them to be delivered directly to the graveside. They seemed so incongruous in church.

We walked past them through the doorway and down the center aisle of the church. Beautiful music filled the air. Margaret Cymanow was chanting "Amazing Grace" with a purity that pierced my heart. For a moment, I forgot that we had requested the song, or that Margaret was the singer. It just seemed to have occurred. Tears gushed from my eyes like water from a spring. We laid the coffin at the foot of the pulpit and took our places standing in the pews.

I can remember very little of what followed. Fitz was there to say the Mass, sharing the pulpit with the parish priest. Despite his solemn countenance, flowing mustache, and bushy halo of curly white hair, Fitz's face was child-like. He compared Christina's grief to the sorrow of Mary. "A mother should never have to bury her son."

My only memory of the remainder of the Mass is of Margaret singing the "Ave Maria," her silver tones blowing on the coals of my grief, fanning them into a fire of such intensity that it seemed to consume all else.

One other memory. When the parish priest asked us to pray for Chris's soul, I thought, *How strange! I've seen his soul and I don't think he needs much help from us.*

At the conclusion of the Mass, we carried the coffin back down the center aisle, through the doorway, past the balloons, down the stairs, and out to the hearse. The balloon plant was placed in the hearse next to the coffin. This was comically difficult. The sandbag seemed to weigh about 50 pounds and each balloon wanted to pop out the back of the hearse. Their bobbing and wiggling reminded me of Chris. It took three men to complete the job.

A procession of cars followed the hearse down Main Street, across the river, behind Four Brothers Pizza, to the far end of the cemetery. A fresh grave had been dug. The coffin was laid alongside it, on the damp earth, and the sandbag holding the balloons was placed next to it. We gathered round the grave in a circle, about 50 people, and Fitz led us in prayer. For the first time, I recognized family and friends who had driven to Great Barrington for the funeral. They had been present in the church, but I had seen almost nothing there.

When prayers were finished, I spoke about the balloons. "We want to celebrate Christopher's Spirit—his radiant smile, his sense of humor, his love of life. The balloons are a symbol of that Spirit. We will release them here, to celebrate the freedom his soul now enjoys."

I knelt on the muddy ground to untie them from the sandbag and distribute them among our family, the children who were present, and some members of the community who had been closest to Chris. The knot was too tight to loosen. Someone handed me a pocketknife with a dull blade and I cut the yellow ribbons that held the balloons and handed them out one by one, the first one going to Jordan, the last one to me. They looked a bit funny. After being cut, each balloon's ribbon was only 12 to 18 inches long, and the free ends were a bit ragged because the blade had been so dull. Not quite the effect I had intended. One of the balloons burst spontaneously. It was hard to know why, because the knife was nowhere near it.

"That one's Christopher's!" exclaimed Jordan.

We released the other 21 balloons all at once. They soared skyward, carried high by gusts of wind, and within a few minutes were all lost from sight.

CHAPTER

6

By Sunday morning the winds had subsided, but the clouds remained, providing a pewter backdrop for the stark branches of the bare oak trees surrounding the farmhouse. Gerry Fitzsimmons had returned to Long Island to plan his next mission. The Cymanows were back in Manhattan singing an early Mass at a Polish church in the East Village. Jon and Jeff had driven with them, and their sons, Paavo and Shimon, had remained with us as company for Jordan. We packed up some of Chris's belongings, those we wanted to save: a favorite sweatshirt, his photo album, the beeswax candles that he lit each night for reciting the Prayer of Saint Francis, which seemed to soothe him. Three weeks after his death, Chris taught me its importance in his life. It's a prayer of transformation.

Lord, make me an instrument of your peace.
Where there is hatred, let me sow love;
Where there is darkness, light;
Where there is sadness, joy;
Where there is despair, hope;
Where there is injury, pardon.
O Divine Master, grant that I
May not so much seek
To be understood, as to understand;
To be comforted, as to comfort;
To be loved, as to love.
For it is in giving that we receive,
In pardoning that we are pardoned,
And in dying that we are born to eternal life.

We left behind Chris's clothes, to be used by those who needed them. His down jacket went to Daniel, who would wear it for five years, until it fell apart. And we left Chris's tapes and records, including the single of "Three Times a Lady," which his roommate had grown to like, and the tape of "Free to Be You and Me," a children's recording made by Marlo Thomas that he had requested as the only present for his 22nd birthday. Years later, Christina and I dissolved into tears as we listened to the words of the title song.

There's a land that I see
Where the children are free.
And I say it ain't far
To this land from where we are.
Take my hand, come with me
Where the children are free.

Come with me—take my hand
And we'll live . . .
In a land
Where the river runs free,
In a land
Through the green country,
In a land
To a shining sea,
And you and me
Are free to be
You and me.

"Chris loved songs like this," Christina whispered. "I can't find words to describe what it must have meant to him. He took it literally. He was always so hopeful. In the face of *anything*, no matter how terrible, he was always optimistic. He must have thought there really was a place like this, just within reach. He could be there and so could everyone he knew. He so loved to be with other people."

Luke presented us with a pastel drawing called *The Yellow Balloon*, which he had made Saturday night after the funeral. In its center rose a volcano, forming an island in the midst of a turbulent sea. White breakers crashed on its shores. Black sharks encircled it. Above it rose a yellow balloon sparkling in the sunlight. A poem went with it, celebrating the balloon's freedom. As we drove away after saying our good-byes, Luke stood by the end of the driveway, watching the car until it was out of sight.

We tried to cheer ourselves by singing. Driving south down the narrow and winding Taconic State Parkway, we sang every song we could remember, with the enthusiastic participation of Shimon and Paavo, until we could sing no more. We entered the northern tip of Manhattan on the Henry Hudson Parkway, took the exit by the 79th Street Boat Basin, and proceeded downtown on Broadway. As we approached Columbus Circle, the traffic became heavy, and I began to regret having chosen that route downtown.

When we stopped for a red light by the New York Coliseum, I gasped in disbelief. Descending toward the car, then hovering in the air at a height of about 10 feet, clearly visible through the windshield, was a yellow balloon.

All five of us saw it. "Look at that!" I exclaimed, needlessly. "There's a yellow balloon!"

"That's mine," piped up Jordan's sweet voice from the back seat. "I know it's mine because I put a mark on it before I let it go!"

My first thought was, *What a coincidence! A child must have lost it in the park.* But I quickly noticed that the yellow ribbon attached to the balloon was only about 12 inches long and had an irregular edge, as if it had been cut with a dull knife. The balloon was obviously spent, about a day old, its skin a bit soft from the loss of helium, not taut and shiny the way a new balloon would look. It bobbed in the air instead of rising up like a freshly minted balloon. By all appearances, this balloon had come from somewhere else to settle at the edge of Columbus Circle.

Christina burst out laughing, "Christopher, you are a wonder!"

The light turned green and the traffic urged us forward. We were in the middle lane; the balloon was clearly out of reach and was drifting away. There was no place to stop. I wanted to retrieve it, but I knew I couldn't. I would have to let it go.

The balloon itself didn't seem to matter anyway. The encounter was what mattered. It felt as if Christopher were there telling me, "I know you, Leo. You question everything. I gave you a glimpse of my Spirit so you would know that I'm not gone, that we are immortal and survive our bodies. But I knew that wouldn't be enough for you. You'd question the vision, doubt your memory, attribute what you saw to the emotional intensity of the moment. So I'm giving you this, an objective sign that I am still with you, evidence that's hard to dispute. Notice how carefully I planned the site: Columbus Circle, named after another Christopher, Cristoforo Colombo. Do you remember how you used to call me 'Cristoforo' and I would laugh with delight at the strange sound it gave my name?"

Driving down Broadway to our apartment on 19th Street, Christina and I were elated. To Jordan, Shimon, and Paavo, it all seemed rather routine. Of course the balloon had followed us from Great Barrington to New York City. Of course Chris had sent it. What could be more natural?

For me, the event was so wonderful it was frightening. I obsessed about the explanation. I checked the wind speed and direction for that day and the day before. I tried to calculate how high a helium-filled balloon would rise before falling, how the rate of its descent would be affected by elevation and air pressure, and how those would interact with the rate at which helium seeped from the balloon. I concluded that I could come up with a naturalistic explanation: yes, it could happen that one of

21 helium-filled balloons released at 2 P.M. on a windy day in Great Barrington, Massachusetts, might alight 24 hours later in New York City, 150 miles away. That was possible, but what were the odds that it would arrive in the exact spot we were passing at the exact moment we passed through? The odds against that were astronomical.

I sought an alternative explanation. This was a detective story. Maybe the balloon didn't come from Great Barrington. Someone living in an apartment near Columbus Circle could have lost a day-old helium balloon through an open window . . . on a cold day in early November . . . and it just happened to be attached to a short, frayed yellow ribbon . . . and it just happened to hover over our car as we returned from a funeral at which we had released identical balloons.

I decided that accepting Jordan's explanation did not require a childlike leap of faith after all. In fact, his theory was simpler and made more sense than any other. In a court of law, it might well have prevailed. This was one of the balloons we had released, and its appearance at Columbus Circle was no coincidence.

CHAPTER

7

Our encounter with the yellow balloon was an incredible, uplifting gift. Like the visit of Christopher's Spirit, it seemed to be a demonstration of the depth of his love that he would show us with such clarity—not once, but twice—that his soul had survived the death of his body. Looking back, I think that the strangest aspect of the whole experience was not the encounter itself, but how little it relieved our grief.

Jordan's blithe acceptance of Christopher's immortality belied the grief he felt at being separated from him. Several months after Chris's death, Christina and I found Jordan lying in bed one night, quietly crying.

"Jordan, what's the matter?" asked Christina, as she sat on the bed and cradled his head in her arms.

"Christopher!" he sobbed. We all lay on the bed together and cried, and then we told stories about the funny and wonderful things Chris used to do. We remembered the time he went to see Jim Henson's movie *The Dark Crystal*. He loved Jim Henson's Muppets, and Henson himself as Kermit the Frog was almost as beloved by Chris as was Big Bird. But *The Dark Crystal* was another matter, an adult fable in the guise of a children's story. About 15 minutes into the film, as the evil birdlike Skeksis stripped the plumes from the dead emperor, Chris suddenly stood up in the theater and announced, "Get me out of here! This is too crazy for me!"

As Jordan grew from childhood into adolescence, he revealed prodigious talent as an artist, poet, and playwright. The content of his work became increasingly dark and sardonic, focusing on suffering, death, and hypocrisy with biting irony and an insight far greater than his years or life experience. When he was 12, I asked him why he was so preoccupied with the dark side of New York City—drugs, alcoholism, violence, and homelessness.

"I like to write about pain, because it's real," he replied earnestly. "You know, Dad, when you're born, you're like a lump of clay. Pain is a knife that shapes you. It makes you who you are."

He looked past me, at a photo of himself with Christopher. At the age of 14, Jordan began a poem about his brother's death. Its main point: five years had done nothing to dull the pain. After I read it, he said to me, "I must have been really numb after Christopher died. I remember, just a few weeks afterward I actually told someone that I had gotten over my brother's death. The truth is, I count the days since he died."

Every day for weeks, and every week for months, Christina and I would talk about the vision we had seen. There was comfort, to be sure, in our perception of Chris's transformation, in the sensation of sublime joyfulness that radiated from his Spirit. But the vision could not replace the child, and the wound remained fresh, full of memories.

His oppositional behaviors now seemed funny, not daunting. There was the December evening when we drove slowly down Fifth Avenue, admiring the Christmas lights at Rockefeller Center and the elaborate window displays across the street at Saks, motorized scenes of an idealized rustic Americana in which life-sized puppets built a snowman, baked cakes, exchanged gifts, and engaged in an endless snowball fight in which no one ever got wet or hurt. Chris could not have cared less. "I wanna see the *Easter* decorations!" he demanded, with just a hint of playfulness. Once when we were driving downtown on Fifth, which is one-way, and he couldn't think of something oppositional to say, he just said, "I wanna go in the other direction!" That ridiculous demand was so quintessentially Christopher, we just burst out laughing. What I learned after his death was that his incessant demand for the opposite was not really a behavioral quirk or an attempt to get attention. It was his reason for being here.

On Thanksgiving Day, three weeks after his death, Chris began to show me its meaning. We had a small family dinner that Thanksgiving, joined by Grandma, who came down from Connecticut, and by Christina's brother

George and his wife, Inge, who drove in from New Jersey. Christopher's absence was palpable. This did not feel like a celebration.

As we set the table, a strange sensation suddenly swept over me. My head began to spin, I felt cold and hot at the same time, and the energy drained out of me.

"I feel like I'm getting the flu," I mumbled, and went back to my bedroom to lie down. My body felt leaden, heavy enough to sink right through the mattress and the pillow. An immense dark cloud filled my brain, bringing with it a profound feeling of depression. I had never felt this way before, even when very ill. I knew this malady was not the flu, but I didn't know what it was.

My mind drifted back to something Christina had just said about Christopher. I had been planning a trip to the Grand Canyon with Christopher and Jordan. We would go in June, as soon as Jordan's school ended, driving cross-country. Chris had never taken a trip as long as that, but he liked riding in the car . . . he loved being with Jordan . . . Jordan loved being with him and, anyway, was easy to travel with, so Chris could get most of my attention. The trip would be a welcome challenge for all of us. Jordan was excited about seeing the Canyon; Chris was just excited about traveling with *us*. To him, the destination was inconsequential. His last words to Christina, spoken gleefully on the telephone two days before his death, were "I can't wait to go on that trip with Leo!"

I had been so involved in my work that many times Chris came second or third or fourth or fifth or barely figured into the equation describing how I spent my time.

Friends and family considered me a devoted father. But I knew that, most of the time, the demands of my work had come first.

As I lay in bed, immobilized by my mysterious illness, the sensation of Christopher's disappointments began to grow inside me, like a giant swell raised by a storm at sea. I was overcome by feelings that appeared to be *his*, as if Chris had suddenly taken control of my mind. The swell of emotion began crashing all around, tossing me about like the surf that breaks after a storm. I had ridden the waves in high surf on many occasions, and the one lesson I had learned was *Don't resist: let them pull you down and wait for release.* Which is what I did now.

I cried Christopher's tears. I felt the frustration that flowed from his handicap as if it were mine. I was inside a boy driven only by love, with the soul of an angel, the wisdom of a sage, and a brain whose wiring was so erratic in its connections that it never seemed to do anything right. I cared most about the people around me, whoever they were. I wanted to engage them, each and every one, in a never-ending dialogue. They fascinated me. I loved them and I wanted them to love me. But I kept doing things that made them angry—and that was part of the fascination, because the anger was a form of dialogue. Then they would turn away, reject me, try to ignore me, try to disengage themselves from my embrace. Sometimes I knew how to say, "Come back. I love you." Most times, I fanned the flames of their anger to renew their dialogue with *me, Christopher.* At those times, I felt so terribly lonely. I never wanted pain, not for me, not for them. But it always seemed to come.

I especially loved my mom. I remembered her hugs and caresses. I hungered for them. So I tormented her more than anyone else. I knew every behavior she couldn't cope with, and I used them all. She hated whining, so I would complain and make endless demands in the whiniest voice I could invent. She needed sleep, so I would bang on the walls of my bedroom at night. She recoiled at waste, so I would break everything I could get my hands on. I wanted her to love me *in spite of* everything I did, with the same total, unconditional love that I felt for her. I loved my brothers. I loved that we were three and then four. How I wanted to be like them! They could do everything. They could read books and signs and write anything they wanted to and draw wonderful pictures. I couldn't draw a straight line. I didn't know what skiing really was, but I knew that they were expert skiers. And they could swim and dance, play tennis and soccer. I kept walking into walls and doors. One winter when Burr Pond froze hard, I ventured onto the ice. Everyone else could skate. I could barely walk. Every part of my life seemed so difficult.

The pounding surf of Christopher's sadness dragged me under until my lungs were about to burst. Then Christina entered the bedroom and I felt myself coming up for air.

"How are you feeling?" she asked tenderly.

"I don't know what's wrong. I feel completely depressed. I can't stop thinking about Christopher. I feel like I'm reliving every disappointment he ever knew."

She lay on the bed and cradled my head in her arms, as if I were a small child. I fell asleep.

I awoke feeling as if a huge foam wall of surf were about to crash on my head. I gasped and dove under it. Closing my eyes, I felt Chris's emotional turmoil tumble over my back and wash away. I was suddenly in a clear space. Christopher's Spirit was with me here. It was not quite the same Spirit I had seen at the moment of his death. The brightness and the power were present, but not the same triumphant joyfulness. It was entering the body of a small, limp marionette, a broken body with some of its strings cut and so small that the Spirit had to shrink or condense in order to enter. Cramming that huge, buoyant Spirit into the small, rigid puppet seemed as hard as shoving the cluster of 22 yellow helium balloons into the back of the hearse.

The image vanished. I was in a twilight zone between sleep and waking, and thoughts were racing through my head. I remembered a thought that had suddenly struck me five years earlier. We were on Martha's Vineyard, and I went out to take a morning run to South Beach. Jordan was three and a half. He threw a tantrum in an attempt to stop me from running and keep me at home. His brothers diverted his attention, playing a game with him so that I could leave for my run in peace. Pacing my stride as I turned onto the road that ran alongside the dunes, I suddenly thought, *How hard it is to be a person!* Here was Jordan, a loving and generous child, with a maturity of understanding that always seemed to surpass his years, living in the body of a small child, feeling the frustrations of a toddler, expressing himself through a tantrum. Life seemed like an endless boot camp, a constant overcoming of who we were to become who we could be.

As I lay in bed, I heard a voice speaking. I was not sure if it came from inside me or from outside, whether it was my voice or Christopher's. I heard it with my brain, not my ears, a thought spoken in silence. "Yes, it is hard to be a person. Life is difficult *on purpose*. It's designed to be difficult, a training ground for the Spirit, harder for some than for others, but easy for no one. We all come from a Holy Place, fragments of God, and we come here to learn one lesson, a lesson of transformation. Alchemy exists. True alchemy—the *only* alchemy—is meeting pain, anger, and hatred, and giving back love."

The voice spoke slowly, repeating each phrase several times, like an echo. As the last echo faded away, I awoke to find myself sitting up in bed. The depression had lifted, and with it went the heaviness in my limbs. I looked at the clock by the side of the bed. Six hours had elapsed since I first fell sick. I stretched my arms. My body felt light as a feather, my mind felt as clear and bright as the blue sky that follows a hurricane.

Chris's voice—or some other voice responsive to his teaching—had just explained to me in no uncertain terms that the purpose of living is the education of the Spirit, and in that education one discipline precedes all others: learning the alchemy that converts anger, hate, and pain into love. I had just spent a harrowing six hours reliving Christopher's education and confronting my own failure to give him comfort—an agony I hoped never to repeat.

I wasn't yet sure what I had learned about myself, but I understood beyond doubt that Chris had been a master alchemist. No one I knew had absorbed so much pain and given forth so much love. Out of love, he had given me an insight into the meaning of life that outstripped anything I deserved.

My heart was full, and tears of gratitude flowed down my cheeks.

CHAPTER

8

How did Christopher's gift change my life? Pretty slowly. In matters of the spirit, I proved to be a very slow learner.

Direct knowledge of immortality robbed death of its fearsomeness. That was the first effect. Not that I became reckless. I didn't ski over cliffs or bodysurf hurricanes or take nighttime strolls in Central Park. I simply lost all fear of dying. Instead of seeing death as the extinction of individual identity, I saw it as the liberation of the individual from the restrictions imposed by the physical body. Life itself was no less valuable. As the unique opportunity for each soul to transform itself, life seemed *more* valuable, with adversity enriching its value rather than detracting from it.

Not that I sought out adversity. There was enough of that in the requirements of daily living—raising a family, treating patients, coping with the medical-care bureaucra-cies and the noise, filth, and crime of New York City. Nor did I need to invent mistakes. I had made so many with no effort at all, in the same unconscious way that Christopher had broken Jon's cuckoo clock. I reflected on the wisdom in his flat refusal to feel any regret: "No, Grandma, I'm not sorry. I had to do that. Because it was a mistake."

If the essential purpose of life was spiritual growth, then making mistakes was a requirement. Christopher's logic was inescapable.

His message was comforting, but it also imposed an immense burden: to confront anger, hatred, and pain and return love. I'd seen Christopher do it, over and over again. I searched for the strength to learn from him.

For the six months that followed Chris's funeral, I cur-tailed all my professional activities. I continued to treat patients, but I stopped writing and giving lectures and spent more time with Christina and Jordan. Every night, we lit one of Christopher's beeswax candles and together recited the Prayer of Saint Francis.

After several months, I returned to my research and teaching activities, with full support and much practical help from Christina and Jonathan. I continued to think about Christopher every day, and my memories of him were so sharp and clear that it truly seemed as if he were still alive. His awkward gait, his beaming smile, his joy-ful enthusiasm, his love of mischief, were as present as if he were still with us. But I had no further encounters with his Spirit. And I began to wonder where Christopher was now.

Christina, on the other hand, often felt Christopher's presence. Sometimes she'd suddenly turn to me and say, "I really miss Christopher. I can't stand it. I can't believe that he's dead. I will never get over it." And then she'd sense him in the room. "It feels like Chris is here with us, right now," she'd say. I'd try to enter into the spirit of those moments, which were fleeting and unpredictable. I was prepared to suspend my skepticism and believe that Chris was always with us, whether I myself could sense it or not, but for me, the feeling remained elusive.

Two years after his death, Christina and the boys were visiting friends in Italy. They had rented a small cottage on the grounds of a 17th-century castle in the hamlet of Montegufoni, about 12 miles southeast of Florence, a city we had visited many times because of our shared love of Italian Renaissance art. August 7 came, and to celebrate their birthday, Jon and Jeff gave a party for friends they had made on previous trips to Florence. There was champagne and pasta, salad, cheese, prosciutto, and focaccia. Music was supplied by Enya's first two albums. A framed photograph of Christopher stood on the shelf of a small bookcase, smiling cheerfully at the celebration.

The small living room was filled with people. The Capelletti family had come up the hill from the nearby village of Baccaiano, where they owned a bakery. Two young men, Gabriele and Fernando, had come down the hill from the village of Montagnana. Nicoletta and Patrizia Corelli had driven out from Florence, where they owned a salon for cutting hair, bringing their boyfriends. Alessandro Boretti, a neighbor of the castle, brought his son Andrea, who was a friend of Jordan's. Wine, music, and spirited conversation all flowed, mingling together. As for Christopher, his picture in its heavy silver frame kept jumping off the shelf of the bookcase and landing on the floor. Each time, the back would pop off the frame and the photograph would fall out. Each time, Christina would pick it up, place the photo inside the frame, replace the backing, and once more set it on the shelf. A few minutes later, it was back on the floor. Had there been a breeze, or dancing, the flight of the photograph could have easily been explained. But there was no breeze and no dancing.

Marta, the matriarch of the Capelletti clan, stared at Christina with a knowing smile. Christopher seemed to be announcing his presence and his desire to be taken off the shelf. It was his birthday too, after all, and he always loved his birthday party. When the photo was placed in the center of the dining table, next to the cake, it stopped jumping.

What Christina missed most about Christopher was the intensity, eagerness, and enthusiasm he brought to those things he loved. When Chris wanted something, his persistence in pursuing it was relentless. *Mom, when we go to the beach could we take that tape? Could we take that tape when we go to the beach, Mom? I really like that tape. I wanna hear the part that goes, "Brothers and sisters, sisters and brothers . . ."* When Chris was involved in something he wanted to be doing, he was totally present; he held back nothing. No vision and no memory could ever substitute for that.

CHAPTER

9

Five years after Christopher's death, I flew to Los Angeles to conduct a workshop on nutritional influences affecting chronic pain. I was tired from overwork. I had intended to stay for five days, bringing my family with me and making this trip a small vacation. Christina, however, had sustained a concussion in a frightening automobile accident at the end of December and was in no shape to travel. So I traveled alone and carried a briefcase full of reading with me onto the plane, but I lacked the energy to read it. Leaving the satchel unopened, I spent the flight dozing, listening to music, and gazing out the window. The northeastern United States had just entered one of the coldest, snowiest, and stormiest winters in memory. In the West, the winter was dry and mild, and as we crossed the Colorado Rockies, the weather below was clear and calm, revealing breathtaking views of white peaks and green forest.

The terrain slowly changed. The color red ruled everywhere. We passed over a red desert with red cliffs and pillars of red rock casting long shadows in the morning sunlight. *How beautiful,* I thought. *I wonder if this is the Painted Desert near the Grand Canyon.*

As if in answer to that question, the pilot's voice blared harshly over the intercom, interrupting the music. "In five minutes, we will cross the Grand Canyon. The north rim will be visible from the right side of the airplane."

What a treat, I thought. *Jordan would have loved this.*

The spectacle on the ground unfolded quickly. The stark sienna-colored soil was slashed with ribbons of ochre, scalloped with white and mahogany. Ravines and chasms deepened and widened, the sun's glare casting shadows of ebony into their corners, giant fir trees sprouting from their walls, adding tufts of green and spruce to the display of color. The ground opened like an exploding firecracker, exposing a billion years of geological strata. As I watched this celebration of the earth, a feeling of sublime peacefulness and intense joy filled my heart. It rose up within me like a fountain being fed by an underground stream, flooding in the springtime, and seemed to carry me outside the airplane.

For the first time in six years, I felt the presence of Christopher's Spirit all around me. His last words to Christina reverberated through my mind:

"I can't wait to go on that trip with Leo!"

I still didn't understand their full significance.

His Spirit stayed with me until the last traces of the Grand Canyon had disappeared from sight behind the starboard wing of the DC-10. I immediately called Christina on the airphone to share this encounter with her. Chris had returned.

That winter was murder in New York. The air was frigid, the sidewalks icy, and the streets narrowed by mounds of dirty snow and frozen brown slush. The aftereffects of concussion left Christina uncertain of her footing on glazed pavement, and she was homebound for much of January and February. The weather was on everyone's mind, dominating all casual conversation.

I spent much of winter preparing for spring. A flurry of scientific meetings dotted my calendar from mid-March to mid-June. Philadelphia, Palm Springs, Minneapolis, London, Washington, D.C. At each one, I was scheduled to present to different groups of physicians, in different forms, the main tenets of my professional work.

One night during the third week of March, I suddenly awakened from a deep sleep at about three in the morning. I shot upright in bed, my heart pounding and a feeling of intense electrical energy pulsing through my body. I sat straight up in bed, startled. A voice was speaking, soundlessly, inside my head.

"You have to tell my story. People need to know."

Christopher!

I sighed and fell back on the pillow. Of course I had to tell his story. It should have been told years ago. Why had I ever thought that I could just keep it to myself?

I lay awake until dawn, planning the outline of a book. It would start with Chris's death and the appearance of his Spirit, a matter-of-fact account of the immortality of the soul. There had been other encounters with departed souls recorded. I would have to research them, consider their plausibility and the supporting evidence.

In the morning, I told Christina about my nocturnal orders from Christopher.

"A book about Chris is a wonderful idea," she said warmly. Then she scrutinized me knowingly. "Keep it simple," she warned. "Just write about Chris."

I planned to start writing upon my return from a symposium in Palm Springs at the beginning of April. As that symposium approached, however, my excitement about the book project was undermined by doubts I had never expected. I had so little time. The spring was filled with meetings. I had allocated the summer to completing a workbook. Once again, there seemed to be no time for Chris.

There was a more profound doubt, however, and this one challenged the very core of my identity. I was accustomed to being the problem-solver, the man in control. All my writing, all my efforts to change the practice of medicine, derived from my attempt to solve concrete, well-defined problems using intellect, reason, the methods of science, and the creative application of systems analysis. Christopher's story had none of those elements. I was literally afraid to write it. If anyone actually read it, who would take my work seriously ever again?

I left for Palm Springs with a rift in my heart that seemed to widen by the day. My agenda and Christopher's could not be reconciled. The strain imposed by this schism was more exhausting than any amount of work. With no change in the objective conditions of my life, excitement for the future turned to discouragement with the present. I wanted to abandon all projects and spend as much time as possible relaxing and having fun. Hiking, skiing, bodysurfing, mountain biking, horseback riding, fiction writing. That would be my new agenda. Taking every aspect of my life so seriously had made me weary.

I arrived in Palm Springs for six days of meetings, accompanied by Jordan. We were looking forward to hot, dry, sunny weather and the end of winter. At one time, I had really cared about this conference. Now all I could think of was the sun.

In between the research symposium and the clinical symposium was a free half-day. I planned to spend it with Jordan seeing wildflowers and climbing rocks in the Mojave Desert.

The night before our excursion to the desert, I was suddenly awakened at three in the morning and once again sat upright in bed, startled, my heart pounding, a feeling of intense electrical energy pulsing through my body. The soundless voice was speaking.

"Tomorrow there will be a revelation in the desert."

I collapsed on the pillow, wide awake and trembling. Nothing like this had ever happened to me in my life, until the middle of March. It had just happened again.

"What now?" I asked of no one in particular.

The Mojave excursion was worse than disappointing. The roads were crowded, there were few wildflowers to be seen, Jordan refused to go rock climbing, and we encountered no wildlife except for one half-starved and mangy coyote. Worst of all, I was attacked by poisonous cholla cacti while trying to photograph them. For the uninitiated, as I was, let me explain that cholla—also known as "jumping"—cacti have spines like sails that make them move in the direction of any object that passes by. For humans or animals, their poison-tipped spines become embedded in the flesh, where they not only produce intense, burning pain but also swelling, making them very difficult to remove.

"I should have researched this trip more thoroughly," I moaned, feeling like a fool. Except for my own lack of foresight, there was no revelation in this desert.

We returned to the resort for the opening of the clinical symposium at about two o'clock. Since I was not scheduled to speak until the next morning, I decided to skip the afternoon's lectures and take a hike by myself in the scruffy, colorless desert that stretched for miles behind the hotel. Equipped with a baseball cap, strong sunglasses, and a full canteen, I set off in search of solitude and peace of mind.

Midafternoon in the hills around Palm Springs feels exactly like the inside of an oven. After walking for 30 minutes along the driest, dustiest trails imaginable and drinking most of the water in my canteen, I began a conversation with myself.

I can't go on like this. Jordan is growing up in front of my eyes. Christina was almost killed in December. I spend all my time working. I'm making the kind of mistakes I never used to make. I'm losing control . . . I don't even want control. I don't have to change the world. I don't have to prove anything. If I don't chill out, I'm going to get sick. I should treat myself as if I were a patient. What is wrong with me, anyway?

I looked up at the searing whiteness of the sky. "Christopher," I said out loud, "what am I supposed to do?"

The inner voice answered promptly. "Follow my lead."

I couldn't believe what I was hearing. "What?" I mumbled. "How can I follow your lead? I'm fifty-one years old, I'm a professional, I have all these projects to sort out. You were just a child, and you died at the age of twenty-two."

"Follow my lead," repeated the soundless voice.

A glimmer of understanding danced before my eyes, shimmering over the sand. "Power and advantage were games you never played," I responded silently. "You were always just yourself . . . and you treated everyone else the same way. You didn't care who was rich or poor, powerful or weak, generous or miserly. Each was an individual, worthy of your attention by the simple virtue of being themselves . . . as if you could sense Divine Presence, struggling to manifest itself in each person, no matter how pathetic or disagreeable."

"Teach and serve," intoned the voice. "Teach and serve."

This was not what I wanted to hear. "I've been teaching and serving for over twenty years," I shot back. "What I want is *out!*" Tears of anger streamed down my dust-covered cheeks. I sat on an outcropping of rock and fanned my face with the baseball cap.

Then came the revelation.

Christopher's Spirit was fully present, every bit as majestic as it had been at the moment of his death, every bit as bright and joyful, but somehow older and more mature.

"*You* are the teacher," I whispered. "And I am to follow you. How did I fail to see that?"

No answer was needed.

I sat for several minutes on the rocks, staring out across the barren hills. I laughed softly. *Maybe this is what Jesus meant,* I thought. *The last shall be first. Okay, Chris, teach and serve. I will follow your lead.*

Lightness filled my being, as if a cool and gentle breeze were sweeping through the desert, lifting the oppressive heat.

I arose from the rock I was sitting on. "Thank you, Chris. Once again."

I walked back to the hotel to find Jordan and accept his invitation to shoot a game of pool.

CHAPTER

10

I honored my speaking commitments for the spring and fall, but decided to postpone all other projects until Christopher's work was done. For once, Chris would come first. His message was more important than mine.

As I prepared to write his story, I marveled at the change that had occurred in my relationship to him since his death. I also marveled at how long the change had taken to come about and how persistent Chris had been in making it happen. I began to wonder how much of Chris's after-death activities had just happened, spontaneously, and how much had been planned in advance.

I thought about his last words to Christina: "I can't wait to go on that trip with Leo!" Which trip did he mean? Was it the drive to the Grand Canyon I had planned for Chris and Jordan, a trip that was canceled by Chris's death, or was it the flight to Los Angeles—City of Angels—that carried me over the Grand Canyon five years later? I had felt his presence very strongly during that flight. It seemed to mark the return of his Spirit into my life and was soon followed by his command that I tell his story. How much had Chris known *in advance*, before his death? Five years before, I would have considered speculation along these lines ridiculous and fanciful. Now I considered it worthy of investigation. The fact of personal immortality made anything possible.

I reflected on what I'd been told about Chris's behavior the morning of his death. It had by all accounts been extraordinary. He seemed to be telling the Lifesharing community, "This is my last day with you. Here is the way I want you to remember me."

When we'd arrived at North Plains Farm to plan Chris's funeral, I had asked about the circumstances surrounding Chris's drowning. There had been only one adult with him on the hike, which was unusual.

"I make it a rule that I never go hiking without a helper," she said to me. "When my helper got sick, I was going to cancel the hike. But Christopher begged to go. That morning he was brilliant. He did all of his chores so well. He was so helpful. At eurhythmy[5] he was able to do all the movements he couldn't do before. It was uncanny, a culmination of everything he had struggled with for the past nine months. It was a special moment. He brought us all together. That's why I let him take the walk. I

---

[5] Eurhythmy is a form of rhythmic, therapeutic exercise that originated within the Waldorf education movement in Switzerland during the 1920s, and was later adapted by the founders of the Camphill movement in England to meet the needs of brain-injured children and adults.

couldn't refuse him. He chose two other boys to go with us. Instead of hiking on the ridge, I chose an easy stroll on a logging road by the highway, near a streambed that was almost dry. The first snow of the season had fallen during the night, about an inch of very wet snow. Chris did not usually pay much attention to scenery, but on that walk he kept telling me how beautiful the snow looked. We were almost back to the van, about fifty yards from the highway. I walked ahead to unlock it. When I turned around, I saw that Frank and Roger were there, but not Christopher. We called his name. There was no answer. We went looking for him off the trail. About ten feet from the edge of the trail, on the other side of some trees, was a ditch through which the stream ran. I saw Chris lying facedown in the stream, in about two inches of water. He wasn't breathing. We pulled him out and called for an ambulance on the CB."

I then learned about Chris's transcendent performance at eurhythmy the morning of his death. Eurhythmy was developed by Rudolph Steiner as an educational tool, an instruction in the expansion of human consciousness through movement. It was adapted by health workers to the treatment of illness and functional disabilities, something akin to dance therapy with symbolic content. Eurhythmy is very much like dance, especially the piece that Chris had finally mastered the morning of November 2, a piece called "Alleluia."

"Alleluia" is about personal growth. When done in a group, it is specifically about the transformation that occurs when an individual joins in community with others. The

dancers stand in a circle, facing inward. Their first movement represents the first sound, "Ah." Hands are clasped
lightly to the breast and then the arms are extended out-
ward as the dancer exhales. The movement reveals a freeing
and an openness to something new, as the dancer now
stands with outstretched arms. The second movement is
like the script form of the small letter "l." The outstretched
arms extend upward and then down, each describing an
ellipse. The movement signifies letting go and taking in.
This is the act of transformation, repeated 10 times during
the exercise. While their arms create the ellipse, the dancers rotate, each turning in a circle. At first the circles are
very small, just large enough to fill the space of the individual dancer. As the "l" movements progress, the circles
enlarge, so that the circle stepped by each dancer begins to
intersect the circles stepped by the dancers on either side.
By the seventh "l," all the circles meet at a point in the
center; the whole pattern is like the petals of a flower. By
the 10th "l," each dancer's circle encompasses the whole
space; everyone is dancing the same circle at the same
time but each is in a different place. To avoid collisions,
each must move at the same pace, completely aware of the
movements of every other dancer. As the piece draws to a
close, each dancer stands erect, in his original place, arms
at his sides, in the shape of an "I." This is the mark of the
individual ego, strengthened by the group, now standing
alone. "Alleluia" ends as it started, with "Ah," a movement
of freeing and openness to change.

In a letter written the day after Christopher died, his
eurhythmy teacher remembered Chris's performance from

the day before. "It was quite remarkable. He was really with us mentally, physically, and emotionally. He made all the appropriate gestures in a beautiful way. He sustained his efforts and concentration with apparent ease and with his own special kind of grace. He seemed so complete, so contented. We will be able to hold the picture he gave us in our memories of him. It was the picture of Christopher at his most dignified, with awareness and poise and that special sparkle that was uniquely his own."

This was a tremendous feat for a young man with severely impaired coordination, depth perception, and balance. Chris was always walking into doors and walls. His face bore more scars than the face of an old prize-fighter. He had stopped a swing with the bridge of his nose at the age of seven and had been so persistent in picking at the scab, despite our herculean attempts to keep it covered and protected, that a mammoth scar deformed it.

When Chris was 15, I had arranged for him to be evaluated at the Gesell Institute of Human Development in New Haven, Connecticut, where I was employed as Director of Medical Research. The visual-function examination revealed that Chris's eyes worked independently of each other. Although his visual acuity was excellent, he lacked binocular vision. Dick Apell, the director of Gesell's vision department, described Chris's visual world as a collage of competing images that must often have seemed random and arbitrary. Christina observed the examination through a one-way mirror. Apell was patient, gentle, and precise. Christopher's behavior was typical of his responses to a formal testing situation. He tried his best to win a star but didn't quite understand the rules. When Apell asked him to describe the pictures on an eye chart, Chris kept asking, hopefully, "Could you give me a clue?"

"Could you give me a clue?" is what I asked Christopher. That request had become a kind of totem for us. I had no way of knowing what Chris knew about his destiny. Was his transcendent behavior the morning of his death a sign? I couldn't begin to answer that question, but I knew that, were I permitted to have the answers, Christopher could give them to me.

My initial encounters with Christopher's Spirit had been uninvited. He had appeared, in one way or another, communicated a message or impression of some sort, and quickly departed. In Palm Springs, however, he had come in response to my plea and had actually answered a question. Would he do so again, and was it a question of *his* readiness, or of *mine*?

On a cool and rainy afternoon in autumn, I walked along the beach between Amagansett and Montauk, at the extreme eastern end of Long Island. The slate-gray waters of the Atlantic curled into four-foot breaking waves that crashed on the soft sand of the shoreline, spewing yards of foam and spray before them. I would have liked to be riding those breakers, but I never swim alone and my only companion was a beautiful 10-month-old husky named Siena, who pulled at her leash to chase seagulls or dug in the sand to unearth skate egg cases and crab claws, which she chewed up voraciously. Like all young huskies, Siena feared the water. Her inexhaustible playfulness, willful stubbornness, and mischievous resistance to training at times reminded us of Christopher. Christina often remarked, after Siena had chewed up her glasses or her clothing, "There's more than a little bit of Chris in that puppy!"

"Christopher," I asked silently, "how can it be that you are so like Siena and yet so like a sage? Who are you really, anyway?" I closed my eyes and waited for a reply.

His voice answered soundlessly, speaking directly to my mind. There were no fireworks, no visions of a Spirit, no electricity in the air, just a voice that I recognized as not being my own, but which I had heard before.

"I'm the same as everyone else," he said. "Don't try to make me more than I am. Every person in the world is like an untrained puppy, and every soul has something to teach."

"Where are you?" I asked quickly.

"That's not an easy question to answer," came the slow, studied reply. "I'm with God, and God is everywhere, all at once."

Christina's uncle, Gerry Cast, who called Christopher "Charlie," used to toss him in the air when Chris was five or six and proclaim, "There's nothin' wrong with my little Charlie. In fact, he's way ahead of all of us." Gerry really meant it. He died during open-heart surgery at the age of 55, when Chris was 14. Were they together again? I wondered. And what did Gerry think of his little Charlie now?

"What about Gerry? Is he there?"

"Of course. Where else would he be?" Chris said, as if the answer should have been obvious. "It's hard to visualize this when you exist as matter, but Spirits are not local, the way that people are. We are not confined to a particular space at a particular time. Space is irrelevant to us. So is time, as you know it. Being material is what keeps *you* in your own place, so to speak. That is the essence of the human problem. Humans are addicted to place. Place is everything, the basis of your entire way of life. Your nationality, your ethnic background, your sex, your religion, your class, your address, your income bracket, your IQ, your SAT scores, your grades, your degree, the title of your job—they're all designed to keep you in your place. Place is the cause of so much misery and heartbreak. Pride of place—and envy of another's—is the root cause of evil. Here, place has no meaning, in any form. There is no hierarchy among angels. Hierarchies were invented in hell, wherever that is." I sensed that he was laughing.

I opened my eyes. I was still standing on the beach. A fine drizzle had dampened my hair and face. Beads of water were dripping from the hem of my nylon shell. The dog was sitting by my feet, chewing on a sandy tennis ball. I did not think I had been in any sort of deep trance. Throughout this silent dialogue, I had been constantly aware of the pounding of the surf. Any distraction—Siena's frantic tug on the leash as a tern swooped by, or the shudder produced when a drop of cold water ran down the back of my neck—instantly halted the discourse. As soon as I focused my mind on it, the voice would resume, sometimes repeating ideas and phrases.

"You wanted to know how prescient I was during life," continued Chris. "That's another tricky question, because there are different ways of knowing. Each soul has a unique agenda, a set of tasks to be completed, a divine imperative, straight from the heart of God, designed to help each of us be our perfect selves. These tasks are known to us before birth, even before conception. We all forget them during infancy and slowly rediscover them throughout the course of life. Whenever you find your path—or stumble across the next segment of it—there's a stirring of memory, a sense of recognition.

"Many souls get so bogged down by the oppressive nature of *place* that they never find the intended path. You on Earth cannot see who they are, because you cannot readily see past the illusion of place. They may be rich or poor, famous or obscure, beautiful or ugly, accomplished or unskilled. It doesn't matter. In missing the intended path, their lives remain unfulfilled. This is sad, but not necessarily tragic. For life exists after death. Our tasks continue after death. It's never too late.

"I was given a great gift. From the earthbound point of view this may seem paradoxical, but I was blessed. In exchange for some paltry physical and mental defects, I was given something rare and precious: ignorance of place and freedom from its tyranny. None of the trappings of place meant a thing to me. When others, addicted to order, crossed my path, I delighted in turning their plans to mayhem. You were no exception, and—you'll notice—I'm still disrupting your plans, even now."

"So, Chris," I asked, "where do we go from here?"

"Ahead of you lies a long, uphill journey," came his disquieting reply, to which he generously added, "with many tribulations. Embrace them. Each is a gift. The secret lies in remembering that plans and schemes lead nowhere. Their success or failure is no concern of yours. Give your full attention to the needs of each day, and resist all temptation to withdraw into that intellectual twilight zone where long ago you built such a comfortable hiding place."

Christopher had not lost his uncanny ability to push the right buttons. "I *have* been trying," I said, a bit defensively. "The progress is slow."

"Slow?" replied Chris, with gentle laughter. "Compared to what, Leo? The age of the universe? After addiction to place, the second greatest bane of humans is confusion about time. You all try to measure it, as if it were a commodity. Some of you see it slipping through your fingers. The rest act as if it belongs to someone else. Physicists and philosophers debate its properties. Is it cyclic or linear? they ask endlessly. In truth, it is neither. For God, and thus for Spirit, there is only one moment, which holds within it all time. At every instant of your earthly life, you have the ability to consciously live in that moment by being fully present in your own life. Children often do so, in their play. My second great fortune was the ability to live in that moment naturally, without effort. Adults not graced with the gift of brain damage need to work much harder at it." I felt him laughing again, with gusto. "But God provides you with many paths of entry. The rapture of music, the stillness of prayer, the passion of love, the caring of the friend and of the helper, the unquenchable laughter of your child-self."

In my mind's eye, I saw the majestic, angelic image of Christopher's Spirit, and within it I saw the boy, sitting down to a plate of apple pancakes at the breakfast table, delirious with joy, singing out at the top of his lungs:

"Mommmyyyyyyyy!"

CHAPTER

11

I spent several months thinking about the illusory nature of space and time and meditating on "God's moment," as Chris had explained it to me. My musing was shattered one cold day in January, when Peter Cymanow was suddenly killed by a speeding taxicab. One moment he was alive—buoyant, optimistic, and full of energy. The next he was gone, instantly eliminated on a Saturday night as he stepped off the curb at Broadway and 106th Street on his way to buy the Sunday *Times*. His wife and sons were in shock. Standing at the brink of an abyss that rent their lives, they drew on the strength of denial. Monday morning Margaret was at work and Shimon and Paavo were at school, trying to go on as if life were a war and loss was to be expected. That was the family ethic: work hard and never look back. Looking back only brought back pain.

Peter Cymanow had grown up in the poverty of Cold War Poland, losing his mother to a mysterious illness at the age of 14 and shortly afterward losing his father to a second wife who resented her stepson. He had lived on a small stipend from the state, virtually homeless, riding the trains around Kraków throughout each night, as the safest and warmest place to study and to sleep. He was fortunately befriended by Margaret, who encouraged him to pursue his music and his education. He majored in theater at the University of Kraków and sang in a student choir. After graduation, he managed a chamber-music ensemble for the Kraków Philharmonic. Margaret studied physics, and later taught it at a girls' high school while singing with a church choir that toured Europe by invitation. Because they had married, they were never allowed to travel together, lest they defect. Helped by friends outside the country, they eventually arranged passage to the U.S., bringing their two young children. Life in New York had been financially difficult but personally triumphant. Three hundred friends attended the funeral Mass at Peter's parish church. Everyone recalled his warmth, generosity, and spontaneity, his resourcefulness and talent. He seemed to us like a born survivor, a man who could always glimpse the cab bearing down on him and deftly step out of its path, under any conditions. He had not seemed destined for an early death.

In the weeks after Peter's death, I began to realize that I was angry. Angry at the cabdriver whose selfish and careless desire to make time had robbed Peter's sons of their father. Angry at myself for all the times I hadn't seen him in the past year. He had worked just two blocks from my office, and we often spoke about meeting after work, but, as usual, I was just too busy and so was he. I was angry at the havoc that constantly trashed the peace I hoped to find. And I was angry at my need for peace.

Peter's death made space and time seem *very* relevant. It was the tragic concordance of space and time that left him dying in the street. I took my distress and confusion to Christopher. In the previous four months, since our encounter on the beach, I'd had no direct communication with him. One evening in late January, as I cleaned up the kitchen after dinner, I remembered the graciousness of Peter's words when he had offered to sing at Chris's funeral. I remembered the anguish in Jordan's face when I told him of Peter's death. "I feel so badly for Shimon and Paavo," Jordan had said. "Paavo's dad was teaching him to play the guitar. Paavo was so happy about it."

"Chris," I thought, "you helped me to understand your own death, but I don't understand Peter's. Was this the freak accident it seemed to be, or was it part of a divine plan?"

"You still don't understand the illusion of *time*," came Chris's reply. "I guess that's not surprising, since you're immersed in it. The concept of planning, you see, implies a progression, a before and after. As long as you're trapped by the everyday notion of *before* and *after*, you can never understand the real nature of things. Time as you know it is at best an approximation that partially explains a limited number of events in a narrow segment of reality. Let go of it."

"I've tried to approach time in the Christopher fashion," I said to him. "It's wonderful, while it lasts, but there is a reality to time, and it rules all living things. If I didn't keep track of time, I couldn't do most of what I have to do, or most of what I like to do. Don't you recall how *you* used to keep track of meals? You would never accept less than three a day, no matter what was happening."

"Time has meaning," Chris acceded, "but only within a very small realm. If you want to understand death, you have to abandon time. In fact, if you want to understand the whole of the physical universe, you have to abandon the notions of time that allow you to manage time on Earth."

I couldn't argue with Chris. Modern physics has reached the same conclusion for its own reasons. The universe cannot be explained using sensible concepts of time and space. The material world *seems* to exist in four dimensions, three spatial and one temporal. But the observed phenomena of the physical universe cannot be described using mathematical models confined to 4 dimensions. At least 10 dimensions appear to be needed, 6 of them pure mathematical abstractions, completely inaccessible to the senses. These models transform time into something quite different from the clocks by which we live and the universe into something quite different from the material world that greets our senses every day.

"My real concern about the nature of time," I said, "is not a pragmatic one. If there is no time, from God's point of view, no before and after, then there is no progress. How do we learn and grow without time? How do we overcome past mistakes?"

"You don't," replied Chris.

"Now I'm really confused," I protested. "Three weeks after your death, you showed me that life is a process of education, of learning to encounter anger and hate and transform it into love. Doesn't the whole idea of transformation imply change, and doesn't change imply time?"

"You didn't fully understand me," he said gently. "There is *no* spiritual self-improvement. You don't perfect yourself. You already *are* perfect, in your own unique way. Everyone is. Your task is to find your perfect self and embrace it, or, more exactly, to stop running away and allow *it* to embrace you. There is no way that human beings, with all the natural fearfulness and selfishness that is their biological birthright, can by their own efforts achieve the alchemy that consistently transforms hate into love. The very attempt to do it will undo it. The harder you try, the more elusive the goal. Stop trying. Let go of time and enter into God's moment. Your perfect self lives there."

The idea of "God's moment" had troubled me since Chris first presented it to me on the beach at Amagansett. It seemed too easy and uncritical; its only requirement, to be fully present in one's own life. I knew of people who had committed acts of violence while in a state of rapture, believing they were "fully present" and filled with divine spirit. Their bliss was demonic, not holy.

"The solution to your problem is quite simple," said Christopher. "It can be found in your own perception that God has values, that all ecstasy is not holy and the human brain can be fooled by the molecules it makes. The way you know God's eternal moment is by what you receive from it. God is love. God's joy is suffused with loving. If you accept those words and follow them to their logical conclusion, you will understand the true nature of the universe more clearly than you ever imagined possible.

"Notice," he continued, "that I did not say, God loves. I said, God *is* love. It would be more precise to say, *God is loving*. Loving requires a kind of separation. It demands other-ness, because loving expresses a relationship between one being and another. There never was and never will be a time when God exists alone, because God is loving and loving requires others. The universe is the fountainhead of other-ness. That is its reason for being, and ours as well. The material world is not just a testing ground for souls on the road to eternity. The material world is essential to its creator. Matter is ideally suited to the creation of other-ness. Matter has a heaviness and a physicality that makes separation possible. In the material world, God creates an infinite number of separate beings, each unique, with its own qualities and attributes, divinely treasured for its uniqueness. That's why there is a physical world. Heaven is not a homogeneous, unconscious, unseparated oneness with God. Heaven reaps the harvest of Earth. In Heaven, the infinite complexity of individual beingness is celebrated with a love of such shattering intensity that matter could never support its energy. *That* is the reason for Heaven."

Chris's words entered my brain all at once, in what seemed like a few seconds. There was no repetition, no pause. This was the quickest interchange we had shared yet. I spent a long time afterward sorting through his words, barely breathing, amazed and confused by what I had just heard. Had Chris just revealed a simple, logical truth or led me into a labyrinth of never-ending complexity? To answer that question and really grasp Christopher's message, I knew I'd have to deepen my understanding of the messenger.

CHAPTER

12

I began to see Christopher's behavior in a new light. Each individual whose life touched his was important to him and he accepted who they were, without judgment. At the same time, he challenged each one, using his uncanny understanding of incongruity. He seemed to understand that many of the adults he dealt with needed to have their egos taken down a notch or two, and Chris took us all on, singly and together, testing everyone to the limits of endurance, himself included.

In *The Road Less Traveled*, Scott Peck tells us that love is not a feeling, but an action; specifically, it is the process of extending oneself to help the spiritual growth of another. Christopher's challenges were the sign of his boundless love, and they always matched the unspoken needs of the person being challenged.

There was Carson, a mute, disfigured young man, who spent his days and nights strapped into a football helmet because he was constantly banging his head into walls. With a laugh and with no trace of mockery, Chris described Carson's room as looking like Swiss cheese, because there were so many holes in the walls. Most people avoided any contact with Carson, but Chris always spoke kindly to him, greeted him every day at least once, shook his hand, making every effort to let Carson know that to Christopher, Carson was a *person*. Chris never stated this, never looked for credit. It was just his way.

There was Sylvia, whose developmental disabilities were compounded by her total intolerance for frustration or criticism. She cried continually, and Chris never tired of comforting and reassuring her.

I learned a lot about Christopher's benevolence from Ginger Manise, a teacher's aide in his school. If the phrase "salt of the earth" describes anyone, it describes Ginger and her husband, Jimmy. I have never met people who radiated straightforward, uncomplicated, unselfconscious good will the way that Ginger and Jimmy did. Chris always rewarded them with his best behavior.

Ginger had been hired to work with Chris one-on-one at the Elizabeth Green School in Newington, Connecticut, when Chris was 12. When I began to write this book, Ginger sent me a letter that included some of her memories. They paint a picture of Christopher that is uniquely Ginger's. I think it explains why she was such a special person in his life.

I remember my first day at Elizabeth Green School with Chris. His teacher told me to just observe him getting off the bus and not to introduce myself. I felt nervous, not knowing what to expect. The bus pulled up and there was Chris, climbing down the stairs with his skinny little legs. It was warm and he was wearing shorts. He loved going to school, so he just looked straight ahead and ran down the hallway, never stopping till he reached his class-room. There, he would stand in the doorway and announce to the teacher: "Here I am, Miss Dick-man," and he would proceed to ask her questions about the school day, what the assignments would be, and what was for lunch that day. When he found out that he had a new aide at school, just for him, he was so excited.

Chris knew the disabilities of the other chil-dren in the class and was always aware if someone in the class was having a problem. Many times he would go up to Eileen and tell her to stop crying because she would be okay. He was always inter-ested in what Jay, John, or Dorothy were doing. If there was ever a goodwill ambassador in that class, it was Chris. He always put everyone else first. He was so considerate.

I loved the way Chris laughed, and the way he would shout when he was happy. He loved to talk about his family and the fact that he had three brothers. He tried so hard on his papers at school because he knew he would be rewarded with a star and he would smile and yell out with such pride.

When I spent time with Chris outside of school, he loved to hold hands and to be held, which wasn't allowed at school. The so-called professionals thought they knew what was best for Chris. They tried to make him into something he wasn't or ever could be. He was a little boy who loved Big Bird, music, and attention.

He could always get attention, usually by being very direct and very polite. It always amazed me the way that shop clerks and waiters would take extra special time to please Chris. One day, Jimmy and I took Chris to A. C. Petersen's after school. Chris stood in the doorway and beamed out, "Do you have donuts?" Well, they didn't, but the manager found a donut for him somewhere. On another day, Kathy and I took Chris to Denny's. It was his birthday and we told the waitress, but, of course, Chris did also. At the end of the meal, when they brought us a cake, not only did all the waitresses come to our table to sing "Happy Birthday," but customers in the restaurant joined in. Well, Chris thought he was just the most popular person in the world. He talked to everyone there. He was so excited. I just loved to watch him with people. He was so social.

Many people who met Chris didn't know how to react to him because he would ask questions or say things that they didn't know how to answer. He was *so honest,* unlike most of us!

Chris was very impulsive and would rush to do things that got him into trouble and landed him in the "Time Out" room. I taught him to say "Excuse me" before he touched anything in the classroom. This would slow him down and give both of us time to evaluate what was on his mind before he acted. Actually, Chris was very polite anyway and also concerned about other people and their feelings. Some days he would come to school very tired and spaced out and could not do anything well, which was not his fault. Instead of "Time out," which served no purpose at that point, I suggested that they put a cot in the other room for Chris to lie down. That usually worked. Sometimes I even managed to sit with him when he was on the cot and we would share secrets and laugh. I know that I became overprotective of Chris and I didn't want him to be in an atmosphere that would hurt him or that he couldn't handle.

Chris had such an impact on the people whose lives he touched. Jimmy and I are both so proud that we had a part in his short life and that he was a very important part of ours.

What struck me most about Ginger's experience of Chris was how different it was from the experience of the Elders of the Lifesharing community, also gentle people of good will.

When we met at the funeral home to share stories about Christopher, they openly discussed how difficult living with Chris had been. They had coped with those days when Chris relentlessly refused to cooperate with the plans or schedules set by others, but the nights were a different matter. There had been nights when Chris would steadfastly refuse to honor anyone's privacy, repeatedly entering the bedrooms of others or banging on the walls or doors from the next room, shrieking. "He really brought me face-to-face with my dark side," said one, obviously reluctant to describe the anger he had felt. "It was frightening."

This was an extraordinary statement among a group of people committed to kindness and patience. It was especially extraordinary considering Christopher's love for the community.

Once, when I asked Chris how he felt about being on the farm, he told me he really liked the people. I asked him what it was that he liked. He replied, thoughtfully, that they were very special. They loved him and wanted him to stay.

I was quite moved by the candor of this community. "There were many occasions when Chris made me see the dark side," I said quickly. "For some reason, I can't remember any of them now. They've vanished from my brain. I just know that there were times when I felt I would do anything just to make him stop and sit quietly. He really showed me what an angry, irrational person I can be."

Others echoed those sentiments. Chris had spent a month living at Buena Vista Farm before moving to North Plain. His behavior there had been terrible. Oppositional in the extreme, he was incorrigible in resisting the routines of the household and violating the privacy of the other residents. Chris became much more cooperative after the head of the household injured himself with an ax, severing tendons in his foot. When we visited Buena Vista at the end of the month, he tried hard to be charitable in his descriptions of Chris's faults.

"He is the most inconsiderate person I have ever met," he explained. "He has absolutely no regard for the rights of other people."

By the time of Chris's death, their relationship had improved. I told the group about Chris's Spirit seen at the time of his death, and one of the Elders revealed a similar vision he had had some months before. "We were at the beach and Chris stepped out of the trailer. He had that quizzical look on his face which asked, 'What kind of trouble can I make now?' Then he turned so that the sun was at his back. I saw something like what you've described. His face was shaded, but there was a brightness to it. It seemed transformed. I had the feeling that a very strong, benevolent force was struggling to manifest itself within him. I could almost see it. When he turned again, that look of trouble was gone from his face. He really tried hard during that trip."

I didn't know what to make of this experience, but it seemed to me that he and I had different perceptions.

The more I thought about it, the more certain I was that the benevolent force, the Being of power and joy, was manifesting itself within Chris at all times, even when he was being the most difficult. By being difficult, Chris was teaching us something about ourselves.

It was Chris's relationship with Luke and Daniel that allowed me to understand the true genius underlying his behavior. This is what I was told about them when I started to write this story. I've changed their names to protect their privacy.

Luke was from a small town near the Canadian border. He had a wife and a baby, little education, and few skills. His life had been scarred by feelings of rejection, loss, and failure since childhood. As a teen, he had watched a friend jump to his death from a rooftop after taking LSD. The boy thought he could fly. Luke panicked and was unable to stop him. He blamed himself for his friend's death and entered a deep depression. Alice, his girlfriend, stayed with him and eventually married him. They drifted south to the Berkshires in search of work.

When Alice started doing housework at North Plain Farm, Luke began hanging around and helping out with chores. The farm became a second home for Luke and he began helping Chris. They were a good team. Chris was always cheerful and full of tricks. Luke was gentle and patient but very persistent in getting Chris to follow through on his tasks. Luke's influence had changed Christopher's attitude toward hiking in the woods. One day in October, as they crossed the ridge behind North Plain Farm, Chris had stopped and pointed to the tree-covered peaks of the Berkshires, shimmering orange and red and yellow in the late-morning sun. "Luke," he said with excitement, "look!" It was the first time that Chris had cared about scenery.

Luke felt that he was worth something to Chris. This may have been the only time in his life that he had felt successful at taking care of someone else. The bond went deeper. In Chris, Luke saw someone his own age who was far more handicapped than he, but who never felt like a failure. Chris's death was devastating to Luke. He seemed to feel lost without him.

Daniel had moved up from Virginia shortly after the founders of Shadowood, Nina and Scott, moved north to Great Barrington. Theirs was a close and complex friendship. Nina had met Daniel the day she, Scott, and their two young children moved to Virginia. As they prepared to unload their U-Haul trailer in pouring rain, Daniel's smiling face popped up from behind a table and asked, "Where does this go?"

Daniel was 13 at the time and already considered an odd, quirky individual in the conservative community in which he lived. Like Luke, Daniel seemed to be a loser. He was smart-mouthed and willfully disobedient to all authority. He cut school most of the time and did so poorly in English that he was placed in a class for the learning disabled, which infuriated him, because he was quite adept at math and science and wrote his own very original poetry. Everyone in his family thought he was crazy, unlike his younger brother, who was an outstanding student and athlete. His mother told Daniel that he was mentally handicapped and would never be able to take care of himself. Not to worry, she'd look after him as long as she lived.

Daniel had few friends his own age and seemed awkward and uneasy with other teens. But he loved small children, perhaps because he had so much in common with them. He was a pied piper of sorts in the neighborhood, his pockets always full of candy that he was happy to give away. Nina's home became his second home and her children his playmates. When her father was hospitalized, and she spent long hours traveling to the hospital in another town, Daniel came over twice a day to cook for the children. He never actually moved in. The freedom to come and go at will meant too much to him. He neither ate nor bathed regularly, and rarely sat through a full meal.

For Nina, there was one story that crystallized the quintessential Daniel:

It snowed. The first snow since her family had moved to town. Daniel was 14 and school was officially closed. He came to Nina's house to take her son Nicholas, then less than three years old, out to play in the snow.

"I'm sorry, Daniel, Nicholas has a fever," said Nina. "I can't let him go out in the snow when he's sick."

"What kind of mother are you?" retorted Daniel. "This is the boy's first snow and you're gonna make him miss it? C'mon, Nicholas, get your clothes on. We're goin' out!"

"You are not taking Nicholas out of this house," Nina insisted. "His temperature is one hundred and three. You'll have to leave if you don't stop."

At those words, Daniel silently walked outside and began gathering up buckets of snow. He marched them inside the house and dumped snow into the bathtub, filling it above the rim. This took about an hour. He walked Nicholas into the bathroom and with him built a snowman, which was placed in the freezer for safekeeping. He then closed the door and the two boys had a snowball fight with the remaining snow. When it had all melted, Daniel came out, put his boots on and said, "You're the mother. You clean it up." And he walked out the door.

Nina saw Daniel almost every day. She read his poetry. She struggled with him to stay in school, but he quit when he turned 16, working at odd jobs that never lasted very long. After Nina brought her family to Great Barrington, Daniel called her every two weeks to say, "I don't miss you." Finally he came, lived in the attic at Shadowood, and began to help build the new kitchen at North Plain.

Daniel connected with Christopher, and it was Chris who pulled Daniel into the life of the community. Chris was a challenge to Daniel. Chris demanded interaction; he thrived on a battle of wills. "Make me do it" was his unspoken response to every command. "You may love me or you may hate me," Chris seemed to say, "but you can never ignore me. No one can be neutral to me!" Daniel, who despised authority, rose to the challenge of getting Chris to cooperate without coercion. Being stubborn and rebellious, he loved Chris's stubbornness. He never battled with Chris or lost his temper. He teased and cajoled, was playful and funny. Once, when they were assigned a job to do together, Chris persistently refused to do his part. He was tired . . . he wanted to lie down . . . he wanted to do something else . . . he wanted to do the job another way, not the way it was supposed to be done. . . . Every sentence and every gesture signaled opposition, and nothing would bring Chris around.

Finally, Daniel proclaimed, "Chris, I'm gettin' so frustrated I'm gonna hafta . . . give you a big kiss right on the mouth!" Which is exactly what he did.

Chris squirmed away. "Don't do that!" he protested with some disgust in his voice. But he started doing his job as fast as he could.

After Chris's funeral, Daniel lingered by the graveside, looking down at the coffin. He was hurting badly and he didn't know what to do with the pain. After 15 minutes, maybe more, he removed his wallet from a pocket and took from it a picture of his mother, the only picture of her that he possessed. It was worn from being handled. For Daniel, this photo was like an icon. Whenever he was hurt, confused, in trouble or pain, he would hold it in his hand and study her face. Leaning down, he placed the photo on Christopher's coffin, then turned and walked away.

I realized that Chris had brought out the best in both Daniel and Luke, by allowing them to help him. They saw they could each make a difference in Chris's life, and that meant a lot to them.

I marveled at Christopher's genius, at his ability to instantly sense what every person thought of himself and devise a strategy to show them that the opposite could also be true. That was his path, to teach through opposition, and he traveled it brilliantly.

CHAPTER

13

By the time I started writing this memoir of Chris, I'd learned to see that his life had been far from incomplete or unfulfilled. He'd lived it flawlessly, always true to his purpose as a teacher, and he had a great deal to teach me. As I thought about his surprising revelations, I realized that they were no more accidental than his life had been, and they weren't intended for me alone. They expressed ancient knowledge, held sacred in many traditions. Even his methods had deep roots. In all cultures, there have been spiritual teachers who were outsiders, jesters, not gurus or professors. They taught by confounding the assumptions and expectations of others. I realized that Christopher had been one of those.

I thought about the moment of his death, when his Spirit appeared to Christina and me. I analyzed what we'd seen: an oblong form with Christopher's face. Encounters with Spirits had been reported before. Had anyone else described a vision like this? I discovered that Christopher's Spirit was identical in form to Rudolph Steiner's depiction of the human soul. Steiner claimed that ancient sages had been able to see this form, which he referred to as "the astral body," and that the ability to see it had been lost in modern cultures as psychic abilities withered away. The last part was an opinion I could wholeheartedly support. I had not a trace of psychic ability. It was only Christopher's determination to reach me that had opened my mind.

I wondered if Christopher had been able to see the Spirit in everyone, while they were still alive. Was that how he could instantly identify what each person needed from him? He showed no self-awareness of any special ability, let alone psychic abilities. He never said anything that would indicate he was seeing things that other people weren't. I wondered if the fragmentation of his vision, explained to us by Dick Apell, was actually a gift. It must have made the world look like a cubist painting. I thought about the purpose of cubism. It's a representation of figures and objects from different perspectives—not just the side facing the viewer—all at the same time. Cubism was an artistic movement intended to present a more complete vision of the world than so-called realism. In a way, it's based on opposites. You don't see just one surface, you see the opposite surface in the same image. Did Christopher's visual handicaps allow him to see opposites in the same image? Did disability help confer on him a unique ability? That would be so Christopher!

Or . . . maybe I was overthinking. Maybe Chris simply saw people with his mind more clearly than with his eyes and perceived the soul more strongly than the body.

I wondered what other knowledge lay hidden within the folds of Christopher's revelations. Was he calling on me to plumb the depths of his teachings for secret insights? It seemed such a strange path for me to follow. I'd built a successful career as a physician and scholar. I was completing my second book, *The Four Pillars of Healing*, a scientific treatise on the nature of health and illness. *Four Pillars* presented concepts of clinical medicine that I'd spent two decades developing and several years writing. It was strongly grounded in scientific research and clinical experience, and filled with citations to the peer-reviewed medical literature. Was Chris asking me to change my path, or helping me hew to it more truly?

As I analyzed Chris's way of being, I found three themes that would guide me through the labyrinth of my mind to the simple truth he wanted me to grasp:

The Gift of the Opposite
The Gift of Presence
The Gift of Timelessness

Opposition—the Gift of the Opposite—lay at the core of Christopher's MO. When it interfered with our plans, it was annoying and sometimes infuriating. When its effects were inconsequential, it just seemed silly. But I'd seen him bestow it with skill and precision to challenge others in ways that could help them grow, emotionally and spiritually. I approached the task of understanding the Gift of the Opposite in the same way I'd approached the vision of Christopher's Spirit. I looked for a precedent, and I realized that the Gift of the Opposite is a lens that focuses an ancient vision of human experience.

I'd learned about the importance of opposites even before Chris was born, during my first year of medical school. We rely on opposites to describe the world in which we live. We understand the qualities we experience by contrasting them with their opposites. High vs. low. Higher vs. lower. Dark vs. light. Up vs. down. Inside vs. outside. Strong vs. weak and stronger vs. weaker. More, less. Expanding, contracting. Better, worse. Opposites supply the building blocks of our consciousness. Knowing how people use opposites is vitally important to understanding what patients experience.

I'd discovered the functional importance of opposites when I'd learned to ski. It's an analogy I sometimes use with patients who are afraid of a treatment I think they need. If you feel that you're skiing too fast and fear that you may lose control, your normal instinct is to hold back, try to slow down. That spells disaster, because holding back shifts your weight backward, allowing your skis to lose contact with the snow and move faster, getting away from your control. The best way to slow down on skis is for your brain to tell your body, "Go faster." Then your shins push forward, your center of gravity shifts forward, your skis grip the snow, and you have more control, not less.

But opposites are not just a product of the human mind. The material world functions through opposites: left vs. right, mass vs. energy, positive vs. negative charges, protons vs. electrons, acid vs. alkaline, oxidation vs. reduction. Opposites lay the foundation for chemistry and physics.

Opposites can be found in nature even when they're not obvious. I'm not sure what the opposite of a tree would be, but the basic structure of a tree revolves around opposites: roots vs. branches. The broader the canopy of branches, the wider and deeper the root structure. They're almost mirror images, and for a good reason. As the branches expand into the air, they lose more water and are more vulnerable to wind, so the roots must expand into the soil to draw more water and to better anchor the entire plant, so it's less likely to be uprooted in a storm. If you're a tree, these opposites are essential for your survival.

Within the spectrum of visible light waves, red and green are opposites. Together they create "white" light. Subtract one from sunlight and the other appears. Before computers changed everything, Christina and I spent several years enjoying the pleasure of black-and-white photography. We'd use red filters to darken greens and green filters to darken reds, in order to enhance contrast.

The most important aspect of opposites, I realized, is not that they exist, but that *they always exist together.* Everything in the universe contains its opposite at all times, even if the opposite is only a potential. That's what Christopher saw in people and struggled so hard to show us. "You see in Carson a mute, severely disabled, brain-damaged, self-injurious creature. I see a human being who deserves the same love and respect as any other person, not just custodial care. You see Luke as a loser who can't find his path in life. I see him as a man who can take care of another human being when the conditions are right. You see yourself as smart and reasonable and compassionate. I can show you how stupid, irrational, and intolerant you are." Christopher's mastery of opposites placed him right in the middle of an understanding of the world that's thousands of years old.

In traditional Chinese culture, this essential understanding is expressed through the relational principles of *yin* and *yang*. Yang is that aspect of being that is warm, expansive, bright, or unfolding. Yin is that aspect of being that is cool, receding, dark, or infolding. Every action, every state, every function is determined by the dance of yin and yang, which creates and permeates all existence. Growth, death, stasis, and change all result from their interplay. At every stage and every moment, one predominates and then recedes as the other dominates.

Writing *The Four Pillars of Healing*, a book that I dedicated to Christopher, I described how the rhythms of yin and yang as they play through the cells and tissues of the human body determine the state of health. Each function of every cell is subject to the influence of yin and yang, a balance of opposites that says, "Calm down. Do less" or "Get active. Do more." In *Four Pillars*, I showed how everyday decisions, such as the food you eat, impact that balance.

In Western culture, the notion of balance among opposites is usually traced back to Heraclitus, a Greek philosopher who lived about 2,500 years ago. He viewed the universe as constantly changing while maintaining an underlying consistency: "Cold things warm up, the hot cools off, wet becomes dry, dry becomes wet." In cryptic sentences, often debated, he compared life to a river. The water flowing through a river is constantly changing, but the river maintains its unique identity. To be a river, in fact, it *must* consist of water that flows, constantly changing.

This is the unity of opposites, the equivalent of yin and yang. It suffuses the philosophies of the Aztecs and the Lakota Sioux and the Dogon people of West Africa. It appears in the New Testament, in statements like "The first shall be last and the last shall be first," an attitude that Christopher seemed to live by. It is the essence of the Prayer of Saint Francis, which meant so much to Chris: "Where there is hatred, let me sow love." Help me be an agent of change who brings out the opposite.

Despite its importance in the New Testament, the unity of opposites was relegated to the sidelines of Western thought for almost 2,000 years, reemerging in the early 19th century through the writings of German philosophers Immanuel Kant and Georg Wilhelm Friedrich Hegel, under the name Dialectics. After talking with Christopher, I traced it forward from there to—of all people—Rudolph Steiner.

In a short essay explaining how readers could develop psychic abilities, Steiner offered surprising advice: Take a walk down a country lane and pay close attention to what you see. Observe nature. Everything is either growing or withering. Perceiving *that*, advises Steiner, is the first step in elevating your consciousness. Steiner's gentle directions reminded me of Bob Dylan's angry lyrics telling us that whatever's not busy being born is busy dying. Christopher went one step further. He revealed that everything is being born and busy dying at the same time. Knowing that is a way to understand God's moment.

So, teaching by example, Christopher had enriched my understanding with the Gift of the Opposite. I'd recognized its ancient roots and its pivotal role in our experience as humans living in the world. I'd found it to be the fundamental organizing principle of biology, chemistry, and physics. I'd used it to better analyze illness and teach my approach to healing. I knew that Chris had applied it masterfully in all his encounters. It made all things possible and warned against complacency. Everything I knew about the Gift of the Opposite felt very satisfying, in an intellectual way. But I wasn't sure how to apply it practically in my own life outside my work.

"Where do I start?" I asked Christopher. "Could you give me a clue?"

He didn't respond, but I saw that the question itself was the answer. I'd approached understanding Christopher's revelations the same way I approached everything else: analyze it, research its history, and define the problem in a way that might lead to a rational solution. By adopting Chris's question to Dr. Apell—"Can you give me a clue?"—I was admitting that my way of doing things was not up to the task, just as Christopher's cubist sense of vision could not help him begin to describe the two-dimensional drawing Apell had flashed on the screen in front of him.

I remembered the words of a psychiatry professor who'd been my preceptor in medical school: "If you want to understand a person's weaknesses, start by looking at their strengths. If you rely on your strengths too much—as people usually do, because that's what works for them—they create your weakness." There it was again, the force of the Opposite. So I made a mental list of my strengths, and I realized that my overreliance on them could have a paralyzing effect.

First came intellect and the analytic strength of my mind. Second came stamina and my ability to keep working and working, physically and mentally, pushing the limits of endurance. Third was objectivity, my desire to see all sides of every problem and find rational solutions based on balancing pros and cons. These were useful professional attributes, but in order to fully live Christopher's teachings, I'd have to stop relying on them and make room for their opposites.

CHAPTER

14

I started with memories. There were times when intellect, objectivity, and stamina had dropped away. Falling in love topped my list, but that was a one-off, far too special to be a model for ordinary life. I could, however, clearly remember two experiences that might help me understand, in a productive fashion, how to connect with the opposites of my greatest strengths: learning how to ski and learning how to sing (or, more correctly, taking voice lessons . . . I'm still not sure I know how to sing).

I began skiing in my late 30s, and I don't think I've ever gone skiing alone. I always skied with my sons. Jon and Jeff were 11 or 12 when I started, and they soon became competitive freestyle skiers. What I found so remarkable about skiing with them was that they were always so much better than I was, no matter how good I became. In fact, when they were teenagers, skiing was the only activity we did together in which they were the authorities. Inherently excellent teachers, they could always see what I was doing wrong and help me do it better. That experience, in which they were the parents and I was the child, was wonderfully refreshing because it was such a potent reversal of our usual relationship.

When I took singing lessons for the first time, at the age of 50, I realized that this was the only time I felt like a novice since learning to ski. Unlike skiing, in which I'd progressed very rapidly, it was clear to me that I'd never want to sing anywhere but in the shower, no matter how many lessons I took. Despite having a resonant speaking voice, I'd never been able to carry a tune well, and my tonal range was extremely limited. The voice teacher was patient, persistent, and forgiving. It felt as if I were back in grammar school. What a novel feeling for a man accustomed to being an expert and authority!

Skiing and singing were activities in which intellect and objectivity were almost worthless and relaxation was the cornerstone of stamina. To commit to them, I had to let go of my greatest strengths and allow something unfamiliar to take their place.

I live in a world and a city in which accomplishment outstrips everything else. What have you done? How far did you go? How high did you rise? These are the judgments made of every person every day. In my medical practice, I treat many successful people, men and women who have risen to the top of their fields. Most apply the same rules to recreation as to work. How fast? How far? How many? How much? I'd run into popular gurus who made it clear to everyone how "evolved" they were. Their "more" exists only as a contrast to someone else's "less." This is a quantitative approach to living that creates emotional and spiritual poverty.

I still spend most of my time as an expert and an authority. But Christopher's teaching invited me to explore another route, which has enriched my life: let go of my strengths and discover the joy and freedom of simply being a novice, an essential step for me in being able to follow his teaching.

I never do this in my work, because my expertise is too important to the health of my patients. But *my* health is important too, and it depends on my ability to play when I'm not working.

Ask any child what's so good about play, and you'll probably get the same response: It's fun. Well, I know how to play and I know how to have fun, but I also know how to turn play into work and banish the fun. My kids had invented a name for that: "torture sports." How could I trust myself not to do the same with being a novice? The truth is, I couldn't. I'd have to trust Christopher and follow his example.

Chris had two ways of doing things. If he didn't want to do them, he simply didn't. If he did want to do them, they would absorb all his attention. John Cubeta, an educational psychologist who had worked closely with Christopher, wrote to us about that quality of total absorption, the Gift of Presence. This is John's description of having lunch with Chris:

Once Chris decided to do something, he plunged into it wholeheartedly. There was nothing half-way about him. One might say there was a certain Zen-like quality to Chris: when he slept he slept; when he ate he ate; when he laughed he laughed. In fact, he taught me how to eat a hamburger.

I had slowly, unconsciously, developed a habit of talking my way through meals. Half the time I wasn't sure what I had eaten, not to mention whether or not it was tasty. One day, I was attempting to have a conversation with Chris after we had just bought a pair of cheeseburgers. I kept trying to get a dialogue going, but it would abruptly end whenever it was Chris's turn to respond. I was starting to get a bit miffed. After all, hadn't I bought the burgers? I finally asked Chris why he didn't answer me when I spoke to him. He continued to eat in silence. Nothing I said seemed to register. Eventually, he swallowed the last bite. Then he said, very plainly, "I didn't want to speak while I was eating," obviously annoyed that something so simple and obvious should require an explanation.

The next time we had lunch together, I watched Chris's expression when he ate his cheeseburger. *Ecstasy!* It was as if he had put all other functions on hold while he concentrated all his energy on experiencing the cheeseburger. The more I thought about it, the more sense it made. Living and working with ideas and concepts all day tends to dissociate us from the physical world by letting our sensing faculties atrophy by inattention. Taking Chris's cue, I practiced the art of "not thinking" whenever I ate something. It worked! Not only does the time seem to stretch, but the food actually tastes better. Through the years, I have tried to extend this principle to other aspects of my life, with some success. To this day, if I find myself eating too fast, I slow down and say to myself, "Chris would never eat a hamburger like that." I smile— as I always do when I think of my friend Chris— then I slow down.

John's note gave me an insight into the Gift of Presence. It's not a state of will. Chris lived it spontaneously. For the rest of us, or at least for John Cubeta and me, the gateway to Presence was recognizing the obstacles to its fulfillment and allowing them to move aside. Today's world is filled with obstacles. From the perspective of Presence, it's a minefield.

The chief obstacle to Presence is the pressure of time, or lack of it. I can remember summer days in my childhood when I would hang out with friends from dawn to dusk doing nothing in particular. We might ride our bikes, swim, gossip, play *Monopoly*. Once all the properties on the board were covered with hotels, we'd inflate the value of *Monopoly* currency and allow each property to build multiple hotels, anything that would keep the game going till nightfall. We didn't care who won. If one player went bankrupt, the others would extend loans. All we cared about was keeping the game going. If I had a sense of time in those days, it seemed like a lake of infinite depth. I could swim and play and dive in that lake without feeling that it would ever end. Most of the kids I see in New York today are so heavily scheduled with programs, activities, and playdates, and so bred into competitive activities, that I fear they may never know that feeling.

Doing nothing is not acceptable in our society, so we don't want to teach our children that it is. Doing nothing is considered a sign of laziness or weakness or decadence. Rest and relaxation have to be earned.

In writing my third book, *The Fat Resistance Diet*, which is about the obesity epidemic, I wanted to answer the question *How much exercise is normal for humans?* I discovered that the daily energy expenditure of Stone Age people was about the same as one to two hours of moderate-intensity exercise. They usually enjoyed a good deal of leisure time, which they would spend hanging out together, often telling stories. That's how they were able to create language, art, and culture.

Modern society has made "doing" an obsession. This has created a new illness, Hurry Sickness. You know you've got this if there's never enough time and you live with a constant state of time urgency and anxiety about everything that has to get done. Hurry Sickness was first identified in the 1970s as a cause of heart attacks. It's a defining characteristic of the so-called type A personality. The other key characteristic of the type A personality is hostility toward people who slow you down—which, for many of the type A's I know, is everyone. What's sad is that people with Hurry Sickness usually believe that they've found the secret to success. We've created a world in which you need to look busy or you're not important.

Several years ago, I went for a massage from a famous teacher and practitioner of shiatsu. I'd been told that it was almost impossible to get an appointment with him and I'd have to see one of his students. But somehow, my medical credentials landed me a treatment by the master himself. I thanked him for making time to see me in his extremely busy schedule.

"I'm not busy," he confided with a serene smile. "I just make sure everyone thinks I am." I couldn't tell if that was truth or marketing, but it definitely got my attention.

How do I get to be not busy? I wondered. As an adult, I've felt as if every moment of my waking life is doubly committed. There's so much to do, so many patients to treat, so much new data to process, and so much processed information to teach. I'd become an expert at multitasking, today's solution to the problem of time pressure. It began to encroach on my family life. How often would Christina look at me knowingly and say, "What were you thinking about? It's not what I was saying."

"Of course I was listening," I'd protest, and then repeat word for word what it was she'd just said. But there was always a several-second delay, the kind of pause you get with a very long-distance phone call. Busted! I'd be listening to her and thinking about one or two things that had to get done or that I'd forgotten to do. She could always tell the difference. "You're just rewinding the tape of what I said and re-listening. You're good at that."

Multitasking seems to be a requirement for success in today's world, but it's not. Time urgency and multitasking are the absolute enemies of Presence. How can you be fully present if you're watching the clock or dividing your attention? In any situation in which the decisions you make impact the outcome, being fully present is essential for success. We can see this clearly with elite athletes, performers, and surgeons. If you're trying to land a flip on the balance beam or remove a brain tumor that's pressing on the optic nerve, anything but your full attention will cause disaster. Maybe that's why we respect people who demonstrate Presence. Watching the Olympics, even as we snack on corn chips and surf the Guide, can connect us vicariously with that quality of Presence, which is so hard to come by in ordinary life.

Christopher, in his usual unique way, had taken things one step further. He exemplified Presence without performance, Being without doing. That was his gift.

I discovered in my work with patients that Presence can be the equivalent of doing. Most of my patients come to see me because of my reputation for being a good diagnostician and knowing how to fix things. They expect me to analyze their problems and come up with a treatment plan. Because they've typically had these problems for years and have seen many other physicians, and because most of them are highly motivated, they recognize that medical treatment is always a work in progress and they want to actively participate in that work. I learned early on that listening is by itself therapeutic, especially for patients with complex chronic multisystem illness. Before

I'd offered an interpretation or opinion, before I'd ordered a single test or prescribed a single treatment, I could see the changes in their faces and bodies simply because they had my full attention.

When I was on the medical faculty at the University of Connecticut, my department chairman once confided in me, "You know, Leo, I've found that giving a patient thirty seconds of undivided attention really makes a difference. We have to teach that to the residents." I didn't know whether to laugh or cry: 30 seconds . . . I was already trying to do much more and it still didn't seem enough. The implications of his statement are both frightening and true. Doctors are under such time pressure and so accustomed to multitasking that even a few seconds of Presence matters. Presence does not always require a great deal of time, but it does require not watching the clock, not attempting to multitask, and not thinking ahead to the actions that I, the doctor, will take.

After organizing my thoughts about Presence, I gave a lecture on what I'd learned to a group of 300 health professionals. One audience member asked a very tough question: "What about the patient you really don't like but who won't go away? You cringe when you see his name in your schedule and his interactions with you are so disagreeable you just want to get him out of the room as quickly as possible?" There was a murmur in the room. We'd all experienced that feeling more than a few times.

I thought about the handful of people I knew who brought out that kind of reaction in me, and I recognized the profound change that Presence can create. "When you're fully present," I answered, "you're not just listening to the other person. You're also listening to yourself, because the encounter always involves both of you. So I start by being aware of my own subjective feelings toward the person. I'm a trained professional whose job it is to help this individual. If I respond to him with aversion, how do other people react who have no special training or responsibility to render care? Then I ask myself, what is it like to be this person, whom most people would prefer to avoid? Often the best thing I can do for him is not to prescribe another medical treatment, but to not be another person who wants to disengage from him."

A colleague approached me as the meeting was breaking for lunch and said, "That was a very sensitive answer to a difficult question."

I smiled, as I always do when I think about Christopher, and replied, "I had a very good teacher. He was much better at it than I am."

CHAPTER

15

As much as Christopher's teachings about the Opposite and about Presence made sense, reinforced each other, and enriched my life, I continued to have trouble applying his views on the nature of time. He'd stated, in no uncertain terms, that time as we know it—chronological time—is an illusion. In reality, he taught, there is only one moment—God's moment—and it contains all time.

I'd encountered this concept before, but I always had a hard time wrapping my head around it. Mystics East and West, grappling with the nature of time, talk about the Eternal Present: God exists outside time. A pretty abstract concept, I thought, because people exist *within* time. We live our lives within time and the chronology of our lives describes how we change, how we grow.

My favorite course in college was devoted to the *bildungsroman*, a German word meaning "a novel of education." The bildungsroman is by definition the story of a young person growing into adulthood and learning to understand the world. The best-known English examples were written by Charles Dickens: *David Copperfield* and *Great Expectations*. The bildungsroman is by nature a chronology of personal growth. There was one that baffled me by suddenly abandoning time and presenting a vision in which all things happen at once: *Siddhartha*, by the German novelist Hermann Hesse, first published in 1922.

For most of its length, *Siddhartha* tells its story like every other bildungsroman. The protagonist, whose Sanskrit name means "he who has found what he searched for," makes many mistakes, learns from them, struggles with loss, and uses his misadventures to develop special skills that enable him to overcome obstacles. Then suddenly, toward the end of the book, for no reason that I could discern, he has a revolutionary vision of the world and his own evolution in it. He sees that time is an illusion and everything happens all at once, even the process of reincarnation. In this vision, every previous incarnation of his soul and every moment of his present life are occurring simultaneously. There is no progression, just one great, jubilant moment. Modern psychologists call this state of mind "simultaneous awareness." Frankly, I just didn't buy it, but Siddhartha's vision was so much like Christopher's revelation that I decided to revisit Hesse's novel.

I was amazed at what I found. After his revolutionary vision, Siddhartha spends his final years as a ferryman and becomes known as a wise man. The wisdom he imparts is that everything contains its opposite within it and that for every true statement, there is an opposite statement that is also true. Two of Christopher's gifts paired in the same novella!

I decided to take a closer look at simultaneous awareness. In order to really grasp its impact, I had to start by examining its opposite, which lies at the core of my understanding of the world. It's called "sequential awareness."

We live in a world that's constantly changing. Change occurs as a function of time. Time that passes—chronological time—keeps moving forward, like an arrow. Living in chronological time, we experience life as a sequence of events. An idea like cause and effect depends upon awareness of the sequence. Sequential awareness is required for analytical thinking. It forms the backbone of science, medicine, law, and language. It's essential for analysis, reasoning, planning, and experimentation. As a doctor taking a medical history, I attempt to unravel the chronology of my patient's illness, the order of events, in order to obtain a clear understanding of the nature of her problems.

My commitment to the arrow of time connects me with who I am. I've always believed in the possibilities of progress. Things can get better. I can help to make them better. I myself can get better. Finding ways to make things better has always felt like the path I was to follow. Improvements don't have to occur on a large scale. They don't even need to be observed by anyone but me. But their absence creates stagnation, which is something I abhor.

The steps I've taken to change the practice of medicine start with instilling and enhancing sequential awareness in those I teach. My main argument with conventional medicine is that it has strayed from its commitment to sequential thinking, because it's come to rely on static concepts of disease.

As I've explained in books, articles, and lectures over the past 30 years, in the conventional medical worldview, people get sick because they contract diseases. Each disease can be understood as its own entity and can be described without regard to the individual person who is sick. The treatment that follows, therefore, is the treatment of the disease, not the person. This notion has become so ossified that every ailment must be described by a code number (the ICD—International Classification of Diseases). Every consultation, examination, and treatment has a code number as well (CPT or Current Procedural Terminology). If the ICD and CPT numbers don't line up, insurance won't cover the expenses and the doctor is susceptible to punitive action. Almost everything that's wrong with medical practice today, from depersonalization of care to excessive reliance on testing, can be traced to this disease model of illness.

For most of my medical career, I've tried to find means through which science could support, rather than suppress, an individualized approach to health, which recognizes that each person's illness is a unique and dynamic process. In *The Four Pillars of Healing*, I described a solution called Person-Centered Diagnosis. It relies on a narrative approach to understanding illness by recognizing the Antecedents, Triggers, and Mediators of disease as they impact each individual patient. In *Four Pillars*, I illustrated its application in detail, with story after story of real people I'd treated.

Person-Centered Diagnosis requires a thorough commitment to sequential thinking: this event happened to this person, and as a result, these next things occurred, which led to that treatment, which had those effects. Knowing what the person was like before the initial event is of crucial importance. With a new patient, I'll sometimes spend half an hour forming a picture of what that person's health was like before getting sick, trying to answer the question *Who was the person in whom this illness occurred?* Although the data gathered are comprehensive and holistic, the mode of thinking—the awareness of events and their connections—is intrinsically sequential and highly dependent upon the clock and the calendar. It's worked so well for so many people that I would never consider moving beyond it.

Christopher had no use for sequential awareness. It was completely irrelevant to the way he lived his life. Christopher's innate mental state seemed to depend on simultaneous awareness, the recognition of multiple events impinging on one another at the same time. Dick Apell at the Gesell Institute reached that conclusion when evaluating Christopher's visual processing. At the time, I didn't understand its significance. Apell found that Christopher's visual world consisted of multiple, sometimes unrelated, images converging on his brain at once. Maybe this was not a disability or even an accident. Maybe it was the expression of the way in which Chris understood the world. Living this way, I thought, it would be natural for Chris to dismiss sequential thinking as illusory. To someone like me, so deeply enmeshed in sequential awareness, so strongly wedded to the arrow of time, Christopher's mental state seemed like chaos and confusion. Which of us was right?

Psychologists who have studied simultaneous awareness never dismiss it lightly. They see in it an instantaneous processing of so many different inputs that the rational executive function of the brain can't possibly sort it all out. They've concluded that simultaneous awareness expresses itself as intuitive thinking. It's the origin of intuition. Intuition is based on simultaneous awareness in the same way that analytical thinking is based on sequential awareness.

According to neuropsychologists, intuition requires a perception of "the whole picture," or the total problem, by seeing all its parts *at once*. Its conclusions may be right or they may be wrong, but the process is instantaneous. Intuition, like Presence, cannot be willed or planned, because there's too much going on at the same moment for the executive functioning of the brain to guide it. I'd never thought of Christopher as being intuitive, but his uncanny ability to instantly sense each person's beliefs about themselves fit the description of intuitive understanding based on simultaneous awareness. Living that way, he'd be perfectly at home in God's moment. I wasn't.

Because Christopher had directed me to follow his lead, I thought I should explore episodes of simultaneous awareness that had been meaningful in my life. I don't generally rely on intuitive thinking, but there have been times when intuition dramatically forced itself on me.

Three months into my internship at Bellevue Hospital, I was called to see a new admission at two in the morning. I'll call her Maria. I quickly reviewed the note written by the physician in the emergency room, who had sent her up to my ward: "26-year-old Cuban-born female with fever, malaise, and fatigue of 48-hours duration. Temperature 101, pulse 96, blood pressure 90/60, grade 2 systolic heart murmur." All other findings were normal, but the ER resident admitted her anyway, with the unconvincing diagnosis of "R/O SBE," which stands for "rule out subacute bacterial endocarditis," an infection of a heart valve that was highly unlikely but impossible to rule out on the spot. From his note, I could see no reason why she couldn't have waited till morning to be admitted.

Then I looked at Maria. She lay on a stretcher moaning softly, her skin mottled like marble—a condition called *livedo reticularis*, which I had never seen before. I'd only read about it in textbooks, and I had no idea what its significance was. Despite my inexperience, I was suddenly sure that this woman was deathly ill and needed to be in the intensive care unit, even if the admitting diagnosis and details of her physical exam did not seem to warrant an ICU admission. So, without delay or further reflection, I grabbed the head of her stretcher and pushed Maria by myself straight to the ICU, where she promptly lost consciousness, went into shock, and almost died. Within 12 hours, the lab tests revealed that she had a severe bacterial infection in her bloodstream, far more catastrophic than SBE, but readily cured with the right antibiotics.

Had I delayed her transport by a few minutes to analyze her condition and formulate a plan, her blood pressure
would have crashed while she was still on the medical ward,
a place with so little staff and supplies during the night
shift that I could not have brought her back before irrepa-
rable damage was done to vital organs. Had I been asked to
justify my decision to move her immediately to the ICU, I
could only have said, "I felt that's what was needed." It was
only the force of intuition—my instantaneous, unreasoned
response to what I saw in front of me, and related thoughts
that I could barely identify—that led me to the right decision. At the moment her moaning stopped and her blood
pressure fell to zero, she had been moved to the only place
in the hospital where she could immediately receive the
treatment she needed to keep her alive.

Maria's survival was an unusual triumph and the subject of much discussion and acclaim at Bellevue. Once the
discussion ended, I rarely thought about the decision that
had saved her life. I just accepted it. Quick reflexes. We
were both lucky. After Christopher's revelations over 20
years later, I reviewed her case for inclusion in *The Four
Pillars of Healing*. I realized that the decision had been
intuitive, not exactly automatic but beyond my conscious
control. It was not based on knowledge or experience—I
had so little then. I couldn't even track all the factors
that led to my actions. They included her glazed expression, her strangely mottled appearance, her soft moaning,
the darkness of the medical ward, its loneliness, my recognition of my own inexperience, and my need at that

moment for the support of a team. An intuitive decision had saved her life.

The power of simultaneous awareness was undeniable, but there was nothing in my saving of Maria or in Christopher's uncanny ability to look into the souls of other people that defied the arrow of time. They both fit comfortably within chronological time. If each intuition, each episode of simultaneous awareness, is like a jewel, they'd be embedded in the arrow. They wouldn't replace it. My arrow would be hard as steel, with occasional jewels as decorations. Christopher's arrow would be made entirely of jewels strung together. And God's moment would be just a metaphor, not a description of a deeper reality.

Then, one summer afternoon, the most harrowing experience of my life crushed the arrow of time. I'd been swimming in heavy surf off Cape Cod for over two hours. Although I was very tired, every time a wave brought me to shore, I'd feel so exhilarated that I'd turn around, dive over the next one, and swim out again.

I've been bodysurfing as long as I can remember. As kids, we used to call it "riding the breakers." As I got older, I added equipment like fins, a bodyboard, and a wet suit. On this particular day, I had no plans to swim, so I had no equipment. I'd taken a long run in the morning and was just planning on relaxing and doing some reading. But the waves reached higher than I'd seen in years and I couldn't resist their lure. As lunchtime approached, I thought of taking one last ride to shore, but noticed that I had actually drifted quite far out. I was about 100 yards from the beach. I didn't worry because there were several other swimmers around me. I failed to notice that they were all about 18 years old. All of a sudden, I noticed that I was alone and farther out. The swells were so high I could barely see the shoreline. I was being pulled out by a strong rip current. I tried swimming parallel to shore, in order to escape the rip. The unthinkable happened. I couldn't move my arms. Paralyzing muscle fatigue set in.

This is really dangerous! I thought. My first instinct was to signal for help, but I knew that if I acted as if I were in trouble, I would panic and drown. My only hope of survival was to stay absolutely calm and tell myself that there was no problem at all, that I could just float out here for a while and appreciate the blueness of the sky and the greenness of the water. I needed my mind to control my brain.

Scientists like Sir Francis Crick believe that the brain creates the mind. There is no separate mind; it's just a derivative of the activity of networks of nerve cells. At that moment, I knew beyond a doubt that brain and mind were separate. My brain wanted me to call for help, but my mind told me the opposite. I knew that my mind had to be in charge or I would die.

The problem with simply floating in the North Atlantic is the coldness of the water. No longer working my muscles hard, I was beginning to lose heat. I could feel muscles tighten and my temperature drop. I couldn't continue this for very long. The situation was not improving, and the thought that I was soon going to drown entered my head. For some reason, I didn't feel connected to that thought. I couldn't argue against it. It just seemed strange. With a jolt, I remembered that Christina and Jordan were on the beach. He'd be playing ball on the sand and she'd be watching him with one eye and the surf with the other.

My detachment evaporated. I couldn't allow myself to drown out here while they watched from the shore. That would be terrible *for them*. It would scar them for the rest of their lives. I felt anxiety rising, cut short by a sudden, remarkable shift in awareness.

"I don't drown out here today," my mind told me. "This is not my time to die." Peace and joy replaced anxiety and fear. I focused my mind on the love I have for my family and thought of nothing else. In a short time, I could feel the surf around me. I was out of the rip and inside the breakers and knew I was safe.

There was nothing supernatural about my survival. The rip current had behaved as rips usually do: sucked me out to sea and released me, so that incoming waves could carry me to shore. I lived because I didn't fight it. That was not remarkable. My clarity of mind, my certainty that this was not how I die—*that's* what was remarkable. Facing extreme peril and driven by deep love, my mind had switched gears, shifting from my usual sequential mode of awareness to a simultaneous mode that allowed me to see my whole life at once, if only for an instant. This moment of awareness was not just a jewel embedded in the arrow of time. It surrounded the arrow.

I realized that my life with Christopher, before and after his death, had always been a dialogue that pitted his way of seeing the world against mine. When I explained that to Christina, she laughed and said, "He won!"

CHAPTER

16

In Hesse's novel, Siddhartha's spiritual mentor is the old ferryman Vasudeva. After Siddhartha's sudden enlightenment, his cosmic vision that everything happens in one moment, Vasudeva tells him that his work is done and he disappears into the forest. As my final conversation with Christopher came to a close, he said to me, "I've told you everything you need to know," and his lessons ended—but not his assignments.

That final conversation started with my asking a question.

"What's it like in Heaven, Chris?" I asked him.

His reply was gleeful. "It's what I always wanted. Everyone is here! *Everyone!* Even you." A shiver ran down my spine.

After taking a deep breath, I probed him further. "What about the evil ones? Where are they? What about . . . Adolf Hitler?"

I sensed a cold darkness. It blew through my mind like a winter wind, chilling me to the bone. I seemed to hear Chris gasping.

"You have to understand the nature of evil," he answered, after a long pause. "Evil originates in consciousness. Many things that happen in the world are perceived as bad, but they are not evil. Some result from the changeable physical states of matter: earthquakes, volcanoes, cyclones, tidal waves. Many more are caused by human ignorance, by desire and arrogance and selfishness, by illusions about the true nature of the world. Stupidity is not evil, however. It is merely a challenge to love. Those of us graced with understanding have the opportunity to lead others from stupidity to wisdom—a truly rewarding activity, as wisdom is so much stronger. As for evil, that's different.

"Human consciousness is unique in allowing a full and complete perception of other-ness. To cherish other-ness, including one's own, is the fundamental purpose of humanity. In this way, we are created in the image of God. Only humans, among all the creatures of the world, possess a consciousness that allows the individuality and uniqueness of every being to be comprehended and loved. That is our reason for existing. Because love, by its nature, is given freely—or not at all—each of us must choose it or reject it, continuously. There are some who willfully and perversely turn against other-ness. Their hatred of others is a crime against God, the only crime against God that is really possible. It may surprise you to know that each of them has a perfect self. In attempting to subvert the purpose for their existence, these pitiful creatures are divided against themselves. Their eternal torment results not from being placed in Hell—there is no such place—but from the schism in their souls, which no love can heal. There is sadness in Heaven for the evil ones. But the freedom to choose, which is the condition for human love, is also the condition that allows them to exist. I can't say that sadness tempers our joy, because it was never any different and never will be."

Sobered by these words, I retreated to my study and sat silently for a long time. I was sorry I had asked about Hitler. The very name left me feeling contaminated. Chris's words about the persistence of evil had depressed me. "So," I thought, "there really is no progress. The world can never be perfected."

"Not in the way you want it to be," replied Christopher. "You know, Leo, you like to tell stories about the way I was in the world, about my amusing, quirky expressions that surprised other people. Well, around here, some of us like to tell stories about the way that you were. The way you thought too much and tried so hard to get everything just right. Lighten up. You're already here, you know."

Epilogue

My conversations with Christopher's Spirit lasted for about a year. Every interaction between us was different, but they were all controlled by him. When I finished writing, I showed my manuscript to a few people—family and friends—and then I stored it away, not sure what to do with it. Many years later, as I was preparing for the release of my fourth book, *The Allergy Solution*, which I had co-written with Jonathan, Christina asked me to locate a copy of "Christopher's book," as we called it. She thought that our new publisher, Hay House, might be the right home for Christopher's wisdom. I'd saved the manuscript in different formats, transferring it from computer to computer as I'd upgraded systems every few years, so I printed a new copy for us to read.

It's hard for me to describe the shattering power of rereading this story. We felt Christopher radiating from the pages with the same brilliance we'd seen in his luminous Spirit at the moment of his death. He was so intensely, indelibly alive. I couldn't believe I'd written those words, and I realized that they'd actually come from Chris. His voice was speaking through the prose much more than mine was. I was a novice translator trying to share the thoughts of a master.

I could see how Christopher organized my education, slowly introducing me to the knowledge he wanted to impart to keep me learning from his teaching, even in his absence. He taught me the true meaning of transcendence. We are so much more than we appear to be. Who we are is not restricted by our physical bodies. We exist even when our bodies do not. We can be robust and powerful and full of grace, even when our bodies are broken or decayed.

I encounter his Spirit almost every day in the patients I treat who suffer from chronic debilitating illness, facing pain and frustration with heart and resilience. I marvel at the children whose smiles and laughter break through whenever their symptoms abate just a little.

I'm constantly amazed by the power of the Opposite. I witness it in my own life and in the world around me. I see strength emerge from weakness, affection from alienation, and health from sickness. It's a source of hope, and it's also a warning. Weakness hides within strength, affection can turn to anger, sickness can overtake health. The Opposite is always present. Living with that awareness keeps me present.

I've discovered that the most important element to Presence is being present with yourself. Each of us deserves our own full attention, a clear and quiet space for being heard. The first part of listening to yourself is asking: Am I the person I want to be? Not in the circumstances of my life, which may be beyond my control, but within myself and my relationships with others? Life gives us so many opportunities to be who we want to be. Without Presence, we're likely to miss them.

I still grapple with Christopher's vision of the universe, trying to reconcile God's moment—the Eternal Present—with the relentless, irreversible march of time that shapes my life. Accepting Christopher's vision has led me to an understanding that is radically and surprisingly different from where I began. In God's moment, there is no loss. Whatever was, still is. Whatever will be, already exists. When I'm able to view life through that lens, an irresistible smile spreads across my face and brings with it an uncanny serenity.

No one who knew Chris would ever have described him as serene. But there was a transcendent calmness that he developed in response to his many disappointments. "You were gonna do it?" he'd ask with a smile when someone let him down. That became his signature reaction. The intention was more important to him than the act. The possibility created his reality.

Christopher's nonlinear thinking has helped me understand how and why we exist.

I think about the creation of the universe, what scientists call the Singularity, the moment when time and everything else began. The scientific notion of the Singularity masks an absurdity: What was present before the beginning?

I've come to realize that the Singularity is *now*. There is no beginning and no end. No before and no after. Heaven and earth, spirit and matter, are unified opposites that together create God's moment. The universe itself is an act of overwhelming love. As Chris so emphatically explained, love exists only among separate beings. Matter is essential for separation, for the existence of the other-ness that allows love to be. That is the reason for its existence, and for ours. Through our love and caring for others, we are immersed in the divine power that creates our world.

I always believed that existence led to consciousness. First came the world and then we found our place in it. Even the Bible seems to agree: "In the beginning God created the heavens and the earth." Adam and Eve came later.

If the universe is an act of love, consciousness is essential for existence. Our own consciousness, as individuals, is part of the Singularity. The universe exists for us to manifest love. What an uplifting opportunity and profound responsibility!

When I stumble under the weight of that responsibility, I remember Christopher's final words of advice: "Lighten up." And I realize that the tool he used to teach others was his imperfection, which is something we all share.

Acknowledgments

To Jon, Jeff, and Jordan for their love and commitment to Christopher and his memory, and for sharing their brother with the world.

Jon, your collaboration with me over the years has meant so much to me. Your intelligence, sensitivity and dedication to our work has moved me deeply.

Jordan, thank you for creating the wonderful video that I've used to present this book. Working under your direction—another novel experience for me—allowed me to appreciate your brilliance and vision as a director.

I also want to thank Jordan and his wife, Jessica, for their helpful suggestions and deep insight into the manuscript.

To Christina, my partner in everything, for her love and encouragement, for reading and listening to every chapter many times, and for bringing Christopher into my life.

To those people who gave me their memories of Christopher for inclusion in this book, especially Ginger and

Jimmy Manise and John Cubeta, and to the members of Great Barrington's Lifesharing community, who not only shared their lives with Chris but shared their stories with me.

To my wonderful editor, Anne Barthel, who grasped the meaning of this book with such clarity and whose advice helped me express my thoughts with greater depth and precision.

ABOUT THE AUTHOR

Photo © Jordan Galland

Dr Leo Galland has received international recognition as a clinician, researcher, educator and bestselling author. A graduate of Harvard University and the New York University School of Medicine, he is listed in America's Top Doctors, Leading Physicians of the World and Who's Who in the World. He has received numerous professional awards, including the Albert Norris Marquis Lifetime Achievement Award from Marquis Who's Who, the Linus Pauling Award from the Institute of Functional Medicine and the Seelig Magnesium Award from the American College of Nutrition.

He has published numerous scientific articles and textbook chapters and been interviewed for *The New York Times*, *The Washington Post*, *Newsweek*, *Good Morning America*, *TODAY*, MSNBC, CNN and Fox News. His last book, *The Allergy Solution*, co-written with his son Jonathan, was the subject of a public television programme of the same name, which has been aired in the USA over a thousand times.

Already Here is his first personal book.

www.drgalland.com

Hay House Titles of Related Interest

YOU CAN HEAL YOUR LIFE, the movie,
starring Louise Hay & Friends
(available as a 1-DVD program, an expanded 2-DVD set,
and an online streaming video)
Learn more at www.hayhouse.com/louise-movie

THE SHIFT, the movie,
starring Dr. Wayne W. Dyer
(available as a 1-DVD program, an expanded 2-DVD set,
and an online streaming video)
Learn more at www.hayhouse.com/the-shift-movie

* * *

*PLAY LIFE MORE BEAUTIFULLY: Reflections on Music, Friendship
& Creativity,* by Seymour Bernstein and Andrew Harvey

*THERE ARE NO GOODBYES: Guidance and Comfort
from Those Who Have Passed,* by Elizabeth Robinson

*THE TRUTH OF SPIRITS: A Medium's Journey
from Panic to Peace,* by Carmel Joy Baird

*WHAT IF THIS IS HEAVEN? How Our Cultural Myths Prevent Us
from Experiencing Heaven on Earth,* by Anita Moorjani

All of the above are available at www.hayhouse.co.uk.

* * *

Hay House Podcasts
Bring Fresh, Free Inspiration Each Week!

Hay House proudly offers a selection of life-changing audio content via our most popular podcasts!

Hay House Meditations Podcast

Features your favorite Hay House authors guiding you through meditations designed to help you relax and rejuvenate. Take their words into your soul and cruise through the week!

Dr. Wayne W. Dyer Podcast

Discover the timeless wisdom of Dr. Wayne W. Dyer, world-renowned spiritual teacher and affectionately known as "the father of motivation." Each week brings some of the best selections from the 10-year span of Dr. Dyer's talk show on HayHouseRadio.com.

Hay House World Summit Podcast

Over 1 million people from 217 countries and territories participate in the massive online event known as the Hay House World Summit. This podcast offers weekly mini-lessons from World Summits past as a taste of what you can hear during the annual event, which occurs each May.

Hay House Radio Podcast

Listen to some of the best moments from HayHouseRadio.com, featuring expert authors such as Dr. Christiane Northrup, Anthony William, Caroline Myss, James Van Praagh, and Doreen Virtue discussing topics such as health, self-healing, motivation, spirituality, positive psychology, and personal development.

Hay House Live Podcast

Enjoy a selection of insightful and inspiring lectures from Hay House Live, an exciting event series that features Hay House authors and leading experts in the fields of alternative health, nutrition, intuitive medicine, success, and more! Feel the electricity of our authors engaging with a live audience, and get motivated to live your best life possible!

Find Hay House podcasts on iTunes, or visit www.HayHouse.com/podcasts for more info.

HAY HOUSE
Look within

Join the conversation about latest products, events, exclusive offers and more.

We'd love to hear from you!